THE GOOD GUIDE:
A Sourcebook for Interpreters, Docents and Tour Guides

The Good Guide

A Sourcebook for Interpreters, Docents and Tour Guides

Alison L. Grinder
E. Sue McCoy

Ironwood Publishing
Scottsdale, Arizona

ISBN 0-932541-00-3

Manufactured in the United States of America

Book Design by Richard F. Smith, RFS Design, Inc.
Phoenix, Arizona

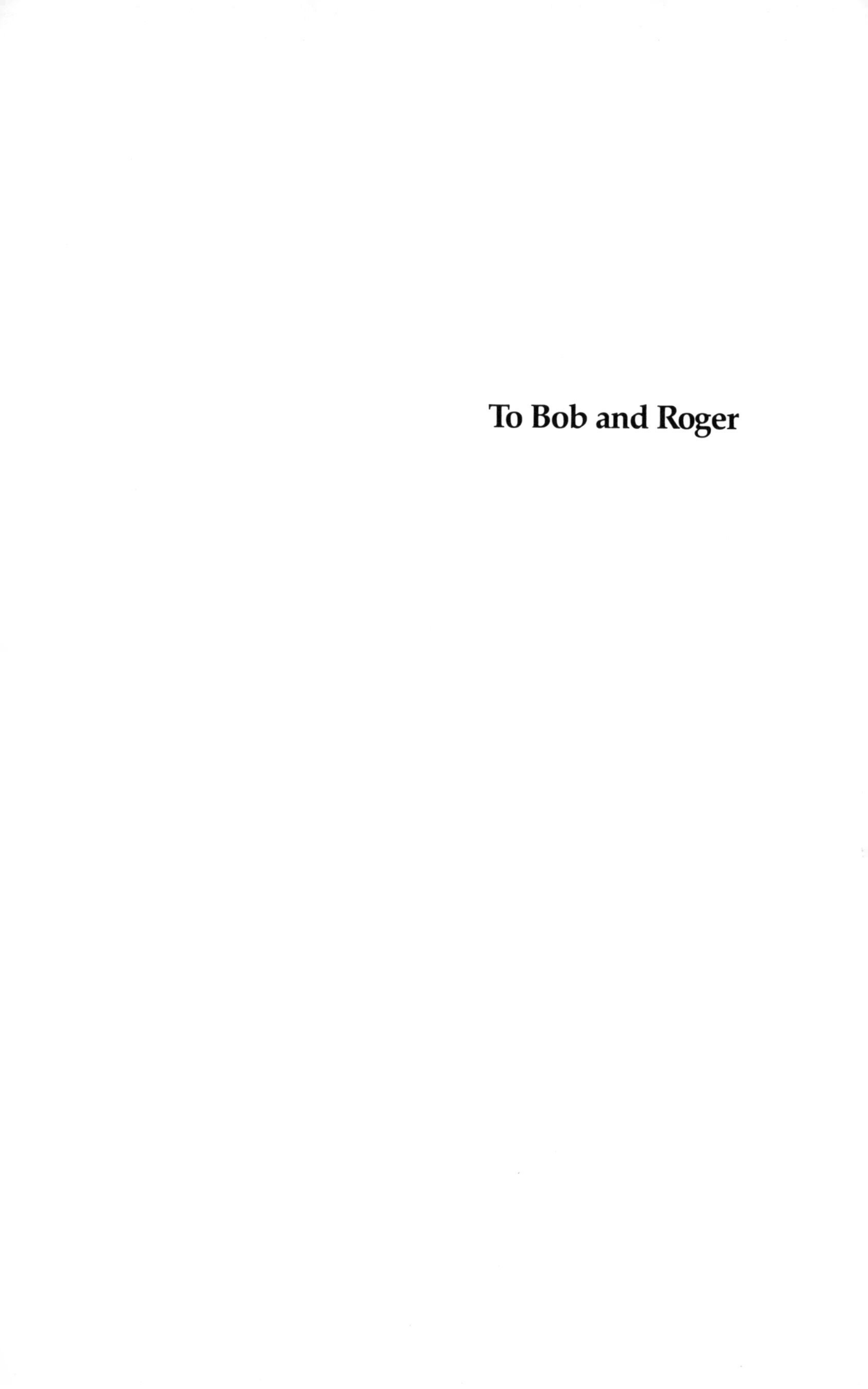

To Bob and Roger

CONTENTS

PART ONE–FOUNDATION FOR INTERPRETATION

CHAPTER ONE
The Interpreter . . . 3
Wanted: A Love of Learning and Teaching . . . 4
What are Tour Guides Expected to Do? . . . 5
The Institution and Staff . . . 6
What is in it for Tour Guides? . . . 8
The Sum of the Parts . . . 8

CHAPTER TWO
The Museum: Past, Present, and Future . . . 11
The History of Museum Education: An Overview . . . 11
Museums as Educational Institutions . . . 15
The Interpreter . . . 19
The Future of Museum Education . . . 19

CHAPTER THREE
How People Learn . . . 22
Overview . . . 22
Learning Defined . . . 23
Three Learning Domains . . . 24
Cognitive . . . 25
Affective . . . 25
Motor . . . 25
Two Basic Descriptions of Learning . . . 26
Stimulus-Response School . . . 26
The Cognitive School . . . 27
Cognitive Development . . . 28
The Four Stages of Cognitive Development–Piaget . . . 29
Information Processing . . . 31
John Dewey: Education and Learning . . . 37

CHAPTER FOUR
Museums and Learning . . . 40
The Museum Experience . . . 40
Barriers to Learning . . . 41
Exhibits–A Primary Source of Learning . . . 42
Stimulation for Learning . . . 42

Learning Environments 43
Learning Structures 43
The Learning Focus 46
Object-Directed 46
Object-Associated 47
Learning Methods For Tours 48

PART TWO–THE INTERPRETIVE PROCESS

CHAPTER FIVE
Techniques of Interpretation 51
Getting Organized 51
The Need for Planning 51
Outline Preparation 52
Tour Background Materials 55
Interpretive Techniques 56
Lecture-Discussion 57
Inquiry-Discussion 60
Guided Discovery 63
Other Tour Techniques 70
Lecture
Guided Involvement
Random
Questioning Strategies 72
Types of Questions 73
Levels of Questions 74
Naming Objects 74
Discriminating Characteristics of Objects and Events 74
Classifying and Grouping Objects and Events 75
Making Inferences 75
Evaluation and Judgement 76
Waiting for Answers 76
Encouraging Visitors' Questions 77
Tour Aids 78
Games 78
Improvisation 78
Hands-on materials 79
Project-directed and Data Retrieval 79
Storytelling 79
Audio-Visual Aids 80
Films 80
Interactive Exhibits 80
Supplemental Tour Information 81
Tour Problems 85

CHAPTER SIX
Audiences: Who's Listening? **90**

School Age Groups 92
Early Childhood, ages 3 to 5 93
Young Children, ages 6 to 7 94
Older Children, ages 8 to 11 96
Early Adolescence, ages 12 to 14 97
Adolescence, ages 14 to 18 100

Mixed Age Groups 102
The Gifted Student 102
Young Adults, ages 18 to 30 104
The Adult Visitor 105
Senior Adults 106
The Family Group 109
Minorities 110
The Handicapped 112
Speech and Language Impairment 112
Hearing Impairment 113
Visual Disabilities 113
Learning Disabilities 114
Mental Retardation 114

Out-of-Town or Foreign Visitors 114

CHAPTER SEVEN
The Personal Guide **117**

Developing a Style 118

Audience Interaction 120

Verbal Communication 122
Saying What We Mean 122
Sentence Structure 123
The Right Words 123
Speaking in Public 123
Enunciation 125
Posture 126
Jokes, Ethnic Comments, Sexist Remarks 126
The Argumentative Visitor 127

Nonverbal Communication: What We Don't Say 128
Body Language 129
Fear Can be Concealed 129
Personal Imagery 130

CHAPTER EIGHT
Putting It All Together **134**

LIST OF TABLES

TABLE ONE: Piaget's Stages of Cognitive Development
Selman's Stages of Social Cognition 33

TABLE TWO: Overview of Audience Characteristics 98

TABLE THREE: Recommended Tour Techniques 108

TABLE FOUR: Tour Planning Guide 138
Sample Tour Planning Guide 139

INTRODUCTION

Public education in museums today is available through guided tours, exhibit labels and signs, written materials, audiovisual programs, interactive exhibits, and classes. Among these educational techniques, guided tours offer visitors the greatest potential for enhancing learning, understanding objects in their larger context, and discovering new avenues of exploration.

The Good Guide has been written to be a sourcebook for both volunteer and staff tour guides and interpreters. Its contents are applicable across a very wide range of settings, from historical sites to such public institutions as museums, national parks, and zoos. Although a strong body of literature has evolved concerning museum interpretation, it has been available mainly to professional museum educators. Consequently, a need has long existed for a comprehensive sourcebook for use by volunteers and staff during both training and touring. Since requirements for each tour differ, tour planning and development must be adjusted accordingly. **The Good Guide: A Sourcebook for Interpreters, Docents, and Tour Guides** provides ways of analyzing and organizing all the components of a tour into a coordinated plan.

The Good Guide is divided into two major sections. Part One reviews the historical background of museum touring and the nature of learning processes. It provides in-depth information about the history of museum education, the characteristics of learning, and the application of learning theories to touring. Part One may be considered a foundation for Part Two, which deals with specific techniques and methods of touring, characteristics of visitor groups, and development of communication skills. Part Two is designed to be particularly useful as a reference when planning tours. Subject matter throughout the book is organized for quick reference. Each chapter discusses issues that we feel the interpreter should understand in order to respond effectively to the ever-increasing need for meaningful education in today's cultural institutions. The techniques described in **The Good Guide** reveal that there are many different influences that affect touring. The techniques are presented with the aim of enabling tour guides to build comprehensive, educational tours. We anticipate, of course, that each museum will adapt the techniques we offer to support its own collections, audiences, and volunteer resources.

Although we emphasize learning as one of the most important elements in touring, we must recognize the danger of getting caught in what has been called the "cognitive trap." Learning in museums can be overemphasized. It is clear that there are many kinds of experiences in museums, as well as learning, that are valid—discovery, reminiscence, exposure to the extraordinary, pleasure, awe, among others. These experiences should not be cast aside in an effort to ensure that visitors attain new knowledge. However, we do feel that one of the primary missions of museums is teaching and stimulating people to further learning.

There are many different types of museums—the familiar history, art, and science museums; then there are planetariums, zoos, preservation sites, national and state parks, botanical gardens, and so on. For the purposes of this sourcebook, we have used the broader term "museum" to represent all of them. The material in **The Good Guide** is applicable in any type of institution. When we refer to objects, we encompass animals, trolley cars, paintings, old manuscripts—anything that is being held for the public to view. The use of the designations "interpreter," "tour guide," and "docent" vary from institution to institution; thus, they are used interchangeably in **The Good Guide.**

We hope that the information we offer about learning, visitors, museum experiences, personal communication skills, and tour techniques will prove to be useful. As "teacher-guides," docents or interpreters, with the assistance of **The Good Guide,** can prepare information in suitable formats for their audiences, select exhibits and objects that best illustrate the objectives of a tour, choose a tour technique that is appropriate for each group, and draw upon a variety of supplemental aids to reinforce learning experiences. When tour guides link good teaching and communication skills with ability to provide interesting and meaningful information, tours will become effective learning experiences. Guides, as master teachers, may draw upon many skills and techniques to help people learn. More importantly, they may encourage people to learn independently and to build upon their own experiences. Museum tour guides can foster in visitors new perceptions of museum collections; thereby, they can assist them in achieving greater cognitive and visual awareness, and in the long-run, enriched, more meaningful lives.

The Good Guide

A Sourcebook for Interpreters, Docents and Tour Guides

PART ONE–FOUNDATION FOR INTERPRETATION

CHAPTER ONE
The Interpreter

Wanted: A Love of Learning and Teaching • What Are Tour Guides Expected to Do? • The Institution and Staff • What Is In it For Tour Guides? • The Sum of The Parts

Museum tour guides are distinguishable from other volunteers by their dedication to learning, teaching and studying. Museums have much to offer those of us who become tour guides. We can choose to contribute in areas of special interest. We can work with visitor groups having specific characteristics or given age levels. Training opportunities open to us interesting areas of museum work. We may extend skills we have and develop new talents. The challenges are appealing; differences among visitors make each experience a new one. The feelings of satisfaction and accomplishment that tour guides experience after working with responsive groups of visitors are hard to duplicate in any other way.

Tour guide, docent, volunteer, interpreter, and instructor are some of the names given to those who "translate," "decode," or explain and describe exhibits. These names identify volunteer educators who meet with the public and provide information to them about the exhibits. The effective educator, however, discloses more than simply exhibit information. As we will learn in the chapters that follow, tour effectiveness is a product of the guide's organization, preparation, and choice of tour strategy, as well as personal style, knowledge, and enthusiasm.

Tour guides in museums today are, for the most part, creative, imaginative, intelligent people who can incite enthusiasm in visitors and offer new insights about our society; they are, in fact, para-professionals. In no other field are volunteers doing such responsible work. They are absolutely essential to museums as guides who interpret exhibits for visitors; they can learn and enrich their own lives along the way.

"The museum docent is neither a teacher nor a curator, an administrator nor a recreation leader, but a combination of all of these and more" (Moore, 1941, p. 24).

WANTED: A LOVE OF LEARNING AND TEACHING

Tour guides' enthusiasm, skillfulness, desire, and willingness to share information can help visitors, young and old, make connections between their own lives and valued artifacts, art objects, and history as represented by museum collections.

After high school or college, many adults are eager for new opportunities to learn. They find that there are subject areas that they neglected earlier or that they have acquired new interests. There are also those activities and interests for which they now have more time. As museum volunteers, they recognize the importance of sharing the cultural assets of their community with visitors and of offering them new perspectives on historical, scientific, and artistic aspects of our cultural heritage. Student groups often are of special interest to tour guides, because cultural and artistic heritage is not an important priority in most school districts; museums, on the other hand, are eager to contribute their resources to helping citizens grow in cultural awareness.

LEARNING IS FUN, BUT IT TAKES TIME

The museum/historic site volunteer is usually expected to serve for a period of a year or more. The challenge to learn more about museum collections and new exhibits, to discover new ways of interpreting exhibits, and to refine touring techniques, keeps the tour guide very busy. When tour guides do not understand something, and if they intend to present that subject matter well, they must find additional time for reading and research.

Learning about the museum's collections is only the beginning of a career as interpreter or tour guide. Interpreters gain new insights as they listen to visitor responses during tours. People who visit museums react to exhibits differently depending upon their educational background, personal experiences, and even momentary physical and emotional states. Their perspectives can be enlightening, and tour guides must be alert to learn from all kinds of situations and to be receptive to new approaches.

LEARNING TO TEACH

It takes more than enthusiasm, dedication, and sufficient time to meet the challenge of today's museum visitors. Audiences come in all sizes and shapes, and museum programs and exhibits are highly varied. All components of a tour, therefore, must fit together. Exhibit interpretation requires different skills than standard teaching situations in schools. Tour guides can assist visitors with "hands-on" or special visitor involvement activities. Some volunteers develop abilities they never dreamed they had—creating environments, storytelling, acting, or conducting experiments. This kind of leadership calls for flexibility, a sense of humor, and an ability to work with different kinds of people.

Tour guides do not bear the entire responsibility for interpreting collections and exhibits. Curators, or other staff, are necessarily involved in researching the collections and gathering information. If an exhibit is on temporary loan to the museum, some information may accompany it. In the process of preparing an exhibit, usually more information is collected than can be used, which enables guides to select from a variety of background materials for specific audiences.

In addition to facts about an exhibit, there are other aspects of tours that affect successful teaching. Selecting the appropriate tour technique for a specific group, for example, is very important. When sifting through information, therefore, the guide's task is to know something about learning, development, group characteristics, communication, tour techniques, and subject matter. It is not as overwhelming as it seems; it is a matter of fitting the pieces together.

WHAT ARE TOUR GUIDES EXPECTED TO DO?

THE SUBJECT MATTER

Museums and other institutions differ in their approach to teaching background material to tour guides. Many offer year-long courses in the discipline of the museum. If the subject matter is limited, or the staff or institution is small, volunteers may be expected to attend only a six-week course, and then, do further work alone. But it is assumed that the subject matter will be mastered before touring begins. Visitors often become uneasy when they sense that guides are uncertain about information.

In addition to the subject matter, tour guides should know about the history and early years of the museum. This information can be used to educate and remind visitors that museums depend upon community support and enthusiasm for their existence. For the out-of-town visitor such information often puts the surroundings, the institution, and the tour in perspective.

COMMUNICATION SKILLS CAN BE LEARNED

Communication skills are essential. One of the greatest benefits of guided tours for visitors is the opportunity to interact with someone who has facts and insights and who can answer questions in understandable ways. Information is communicated more effectively from person to person, especially when it relates specifically to the learner's own experiences. It is the latter element that makes the interpretation memorable and meaningful. Electronic interpretation, through visual images (TV or slides), can help make people more receptive to exhibits. It can thus augment exhibit interpretation by volunteers. The Heard Museum in Phoenix, for example, offers visitors a multi-image slide presentation about Native American cultures and environments (narrated by Native Americans) prior to entering a comprehensive exhibit. Such media presentations provide background for visitors whether or not they participate in guided tours.

It is not necessary to be a public speaker or professional entertainer to be a successful guide. Appropriate skills can be developed over time, and it is helpful in learning them to observe others who are able to communicate well with visitors. **The Good Guide: A Sourcebook for Interpreters, Docents and Tour Guides** will describe several successful methods for sharing information effectively.

THE INSTITUTION AND STAFF

STAFF EXPECTATIONS

Museums, historic sites, national parks, and all other institutions have expectations for their volunteers. Guides are expected to conduct themselves in a professional manner. They have duties to perform, and they are relied upon to do them well. They are also expected to complete the training course by attending classes and lectures. They have an obligation to do their best work and to donate time and good will in return for the training and staff time the museum gives them.

STAFF RELATIONSHIPS

The curators and other members of a museum staff are the major sources of exhibit and background information for guides as they prepare for a tour. However, the individuals have many other duties and cannot always be available to discuss exhibit issues or answer questions. Many institutions feel that the volunteer coordinator or trainer, if there is one, should serve as an intermediary for questions; others find that putting several inquiries together in written form allows the curator to work with tour guides efficiently. Of course, tour guides should expect that a curator, educator, or a staff member will directly address particularly important aspects of tour preparation—content, expectations of the institution in regard to exhibit objectives, effective interpretation, teaching strategies, and so forth. Staff should be made to feel that the volunteers are supplementing their functions and are not interfering with their jobs. It is the responsibility of the institution to establish proper relations among staff and volunteers.

VOLUNTEER EXPECTATIONS

Volunteers should expect that their program will have the full support of the administration and staff. They should be assured that they will be properly supervised, thoroughly trained, and constructively evaluated. Interpreters should be able to understand their roles clearly and to anticipate that such roles will fit their skills and abilities. Certainly, it is hoped that satisfactory working conditions, appropriate incentives, and ample recognition will be provided.

VOLUNTEER TRAINING

Volunteers fill many roles as tour guides. They must be competent educators, interpreters, promoters, publicists, and actors. They will bring many skills to their volunteer job, but most of them find that they want and need the kind of task-specific training that will prepare them for their responsibilities as interpreters.

Training classes may vary in length, depending upon the museum or historic site. Following the training sessions, volunteers are usually asked to serve at least one year as guides. The size of the museum and the scope of the collection often determines the nature of volunteer training. Perhaps one period of art is exhibited in a wing by itself, and its interpretation may require as much training as all the collections of a smaller museum. After a year or more of touring in a large institution, interpreters may become conversant about several different collections. In state parks, botanical gardens, and zoos, it is often necessary for guides to discuss botany, geology, zoology, geography, and anthropology during a single guided tour. Bus tour and city guides may discuss only specific areas or buildings, but they will need background information about both the history and the flora and fauna of the area in order to field questions.

Most institutions use staff curators or visiting lecturers to teach guide or docent classes. Much of the interpreter's knowledge, however, will be learned outside of class time in the community library, at a nearby university, or, if resources are available, at the museum itself. Where small museums are concerned, tour guides often have to piece together techniques, skills, and information by themselves. Some museums prefer to have guides give prewritten presentations or "canned tours." These are not good educational practices because they inhibit spontaneous discussion during the tour.

WHAT IS IN IT FOR TOUR GUIDES?

Interpreters find satisfactions and rewards in many different settings. Imagine how satisfying it would be to serve as a tour guide, for example, in a history museum with a group of young elementary school children; at a contemporary art exhibit with high school students, talking about the artist's interpretation; at a restored prairie in the mid-west leading a walk for young adults; and at an untouched desert, taking a retired group through when the spring flowers are in bloom. Consider the pleasures of other interpreters who might be exploring a coastal environment with a group of scouts, or explaining to inner-city youngsters what a Foucault pendulum is, how a lighthouse works, or why a Great Horned Owl sees well at night. Sometimes guides may find themselves involved in a blacksmithing project with interested tourists, sometimes in a discussion about the interior of a restored house.

It is impossible to determine what leads thousands of people to become volunteer tour guides for visitors at museums, historic sites, and national parks. There are as many motives for their work as there are volunteers. Many volunteers find that they have enriched their own lives by learning with people who have similar interests. They enjoy being active in interesting work. Most volunteers find it a wonderful way to spend time. We can all recall some of the guides or volunteers whom we have met, perhaps a volunteer at the Roosevelt Library in Hyde Park, a lecturer at Glacier National Park, a docent at the Los Angeles County Museum, or a demonstrator at the Boston Museum of Science. The tours may have differed in style and content, but they represented people doing what they loved to do, sharing information and meeting people while they, too, are learning.

THE SUM OF THE PARTS

To put together the whole interpretive package—the preparation, content, visitor identification, and so on, is an easy procedure, once the components are identified and defined, as they will be in the chapters to follow. Much depends on volunteers themselves and what they bring to the task. The following points summarize our responsibilities as interpreters, docents, or tour guides.

1. We must know ourselves, our personalities, our strengths and our weaknesses. We must acknowledge the extent of our dedication to the subject matter, the museum, and the community, and then, make commitments that we can keep.
2. We should maintain a professional attitude, keeping a mature outlook that does not reveal personal opinions or personal problems. We must be sure to carry out, in a willing manner, the responsibilities that are assigned to us.
3. We must learn the educational philosophy of the institution for which we are conducting tours.
4. We should understand how different people learn, since guiding tours of a museum, historic site, or national park is, in fact, teaching.
5. We should understand museum visitors, their general intellectual abilities, their limitations, and their possible physical disabilities.
6. We should understand all facets of interpersonal communication skills, and adapt our bodies and minds to the task of getting our message across.
7. We must know our subject—an overview of art history, natural history, science, anthropology, or history—whatever subjects are emphasized in our institution.
8. We must have detailed information about the specific subject or exhibit we are touring.
9. We should have interpretive strategies that will enable us to know exactly how to get a point across.
10. We should be ready to change direction or react to an unexpected situation whenever problems arise.
11. We should be gracious, friendly, and warm with all visitors.

(Interpretation) is an information service . . . a guiding service . . . an educational service . . . an entertainment service . . . a propaganda service . . . an inspira-

tional service. Interpretation aims at giving people new understanding, new insights, new enthusiasm, new interests. A good interpreter is a sort of Pied Piper, leading people easily into new and fascinating worlds that their senses never really penetrated before. He needs three basic attitudes: knowledge, enthusiasm, and a bit of the common touch (Edwards, 1976, p. 4).

REFERENCES

Edwards, Y. (1976). In G. W. Sharpe **Interpreting the Environment.** New York: John Wiley and Sons.

Moore, E. M. (1941). **Youth in Museums.** Philadelphia: University of Pennsylvania Press.

CHAPTER TWO
The Museum: Past, Present and Future

The History of Museum Education: An Overview • Museums as Educational Institutions • The Interpreter • The Future of Museum Education

THE HISTORY OF MUSEUM EDUCATION: AN OVERVIEW

Early museum collections were not intended for public display; they simply reflected the personal collecting interests of individuals. One of the earliest such museums in the world was the Ashmolean in Oxford, England, which was established in 1683. Over one hundred and fifty years later, the British "museum act" of 1845 permitted town councils to use public funds to establish and maintain museums. From this legislation many city and town museums were started (Winstanley, 1967). During the Victorian era the general public became interested in museums. In 1852, one of the earliest public museums, the renowned Victoria and Albert Museum, was founded in London. It specialized in decorative arts and crafts, and it is thought of today as the first of the "modern" museums which had public education as one of its objectives.

One of the earliest museums in North America was founded in Philadelphia about 1786 by the painter Charles Wilson Peale. He tried to represent the "universe of nature" (scientific knowledge), and he had the idea of presenting "universal knowledge," as do some of our museums today (Richardson, 1963, p. 42).

Fees were charged at most museums in the 19th century for the purpose of keeping unacceptable visitors out, as museums were not always considered appropriate places for the general public to visit. However, for those who did enter, information about exhibits was usually available. Occasionally, directors and staff members led groups through the exhibitions, providing scholarly information along the way. When public museums were founded throughout the United States (particularly in the East), their first priorities were other than public education. Museums, it was thought, should be centers of learning for students and scholars. Generally, museum education then was a by-product—not an objective. However, some saw museums as places where the general public could "improve themselves." Despite this stirring of public awareness, museums, in fact, did not exist for immigrants, laborers, or the poor of the cities. A few museum leaders, however, speculated about the influence of museums on people. They believed that in museums "the diffusion of art in its higher forms of beauty would tend directly to humanize, to educate and refine a practical and laborious people" (Tomkins, 1970, p. 16). Museums were seen by these leaders as having a civilizing influence on the populace. Exhibits should be "enjoyed," particularly in art museums, and it was hoped that they would improve public taste and character (Silver, 1978).

A dialogue begun among art museum leaders provided a focus for community education, a goal that was eventually to be accepted by most museums. At first, contrasting viewpoints regarding the aesthetic versus the social purpose of art museums were championed by Benjamin Ives Gilman and John Cotton Dana. Gilman, Secretary of the Boston Museum of Fine Arts from 1893-1925, felt that the museum's purpose should be that of uplifting popular morals and refining tastes. The museum was "primarily an institution of culture and only secondarily a seat of learning" (Gilman, 1918, p. xi). To this day, some museums support Gilman's original idea that exposure to art, in and of itself, helps make people better members of society. Gilman's innovative volunteer docent program at the Boston Museum did help fulfill his ideas, in a small way, to improve society and to utilize available talent; the docent tours also enabled the community at large to be aware of the collections at the Fine Arts Museum. Whether they raised any of the people of Boston to Gilman's artistic and moral standards is questionable. On the other hand, John Cotton Dana, founder and director of The Newark Museum (1909-1929) felt that "the primary importance of a work of art was as a carrier of ideas and information; the work was to be valued as much as a social document as an aesthetic object" (Bay, 1984, p. 4). The task of the museum was to educate—to bring information and ideas to the people. Museums held the "stuff" of civilization and, therefore, should not only preserve objects but also communicate their meaning to society. Although both Gilman and Dana urged that museums be used to "socialize" people, Gilman felt exposure alone was sufficient; Dana urged that museums communicate information and a perspective to life, thus giving the objects meaning.

Museum staffs were largely male in nineteenth-century America; most of them had independent resources and were well educated. As museums grew in number after the turn of the century, administrators began to recognize that trained personnel were needed, although there was disagreement at the time about what kind of training was appropriate. Some felt a need for people to learn the technical skills that would enable them to prepare exhibits and to practice conservation of objects. Others supported art history courses, a strong foundation in a specific area, and general administrative preparation. Dana emphasized the responsibility of museums to educate people and, therefore, he began an apprenticeship program that stressed instruction about all facets of museum functions, including those of education. Students had opportunity to work in every department of The Newark Museum, for example, carrying out Dana's belief that museums needed experienced people in education and other phases of museum work. Thus, at the turn of the century, museum leaders began to change their institutions from being mainly the caretakers of collections. They began to prepare them for service to the broader community.

However, emerging museum policy was influenced by the forces of society as well as by these early leaders in the museum field. When museums began admitting the general public and providing exhibits that were of interest to it, they were responding, in part, to a fear that the Industrial Age would change society and that handcrafted art objects would no longer be appreciated. The Victoria and Albert Museum, with its emphasis on the decorative arts, for example, was one such museum. Art museum policy, therefore, moved beyond research and storage of objects when museums began to use their collections to stimulate and inspire contemporary artisans. Some of the leading museum art schools were founded solely for the purpose of educating and stimulating artists and craftsmen of the new age (Newsom and Silver, 1978).

The beginning of adult education is found in the workshops and art classes that were given for and by those without work during the depression of the 1930s. The WPA, in assisting the unemployed, helped bring adult education to the fore. Money allocated by the New Deal and educational foundations also supported education of all kinds. While the emphasis was on art and artists, many urban museums opened their doors free of charge to the public, hoping that exposure to the exhibits, workshops, and free lectures would at least provide some kind of education and diversion for the unemployed. Some museums were thus beginning to make public education an important function, and step by step, they were abandoning Gilman's elitist ideas. However, there were those who feared the burdens which educational activities imposed. "The increasing pressure on museums to base their existence as public institutions on educational services is creating situations where continued support has to be sought in terms of specific returns in popular learning" (Adam, 1939, p. 31).However, everyone still did not see education in conjunction with exhibits as one of the main functions of museums. "The place of lecturers, docents, and planned activities under competent instructors is incidental to the main work of the museum—that of collection, arrangement and public display" (Adam, 1939, p. 32). The debate, therefore, continued about the function of museums and what kind of education, if any, was appropriate.

Nevertheless, genuine movement in museum philosophy and purpose really shifted to the side of more educational services, probably because of the increased emphasis since the early 1900s on educational programming and the greater involvement of the public in policy. In a 1939 report, the president of the Carnegie Foundation, Frederick E. Keppel, stated (cited in Silver, 1978) that "the shift in emphasis from the custodial function of the American Museum to its opportunities for educational and other services is now nearly everywhere an accomplished fact" (p. 16). It had now been recognized that education was an important function; attractive exhibits with better labels, and tours by docents, however, were only the beginning of growing attention to educational methods.

The real change toward more sophisticated and planned educational activities occurred during the 1960s and 1970s. The public became more sensitive and responsive to discrimination against the disabled, women, and other races and cultures. Minorities began to challenge the museum's elitism and its focus on Western European heritage. The Third World suddenly existed. Museums eagerly responded to this new and demanding consciousness by becoming accessible to the disabled, by creating outreach programs that involved students and adults who otherwise might not come into museums, by setting up satellite museums, and by teaching with cultural approaches—a rebirth of John Cotton Dana's exhortations. Museums entered further into the mainstream of life by helping people understand their world and the cultures which had contributed to it. New museums and art centers came into existence in response to the increasing interest in cultural pluralism. The museums were beginning to program from a heightened awareness of their social responsibility. Museums were now educating in a number of ways: factual information on labels, workshops, guided tours, outreach programs, and exhibits that involved visitors both physically and intellectually.

The American Association of Museums, in 1967, put its authority behind increased educational services by urging museums to "place budgetary importance" upon education and community relations, and to find "new and nontraditional audiences" (Booth et al, 1982). In response to this entreaty, and to pressure for exciting exhibits which would attract audiences, museums scheduled exhibits that emphasized public appeal and educational value. These changes through the years have evolved into a consolidation of services and a refinement of programs.

Science and children's museums have been instrumental in fostering change in the static display of exhibits. Adults and children delight in exhibit interaction, and the Boston Children's Museum, San Francisco's Exploratorium, and Old Sturbridge Village emerged as leaders in the "new" museum education (Bay, 1984). They attempted to do away with uninteresting, nonparticipatory exhibits, which often put an entire collection in a single room. For example, when children are presented with thousands of insects on pins lined up in glass cases, learning is tenuous at best. Interest in such an exhibit must be generated by the tour guide, which is a difficult task since the display itself does not attract the attention of the children.

Thus, museums have come far in ways that were not even contemplated when the 1939 Keppel Report took note of the new emphasis on education. The 1984 Commission on Museums for a New Century has made education one of its top priorities. Museums have employed more staff to meet higher design and editorial standards for brochures, bulletins, and scholarly publications (Wertz, 1984). They have hired educators either with training in education or with classroom teaching experience. Many of them have begun to use accepted educational methods in their programming and touring, in part, by integrating the learning stages of Piaget and by restoring Dewey's methods of hands-on activities. The public has responded to the new exhibits and programs by visiting museums in larger numbers than ever before.

The trend toward the democratization of museums, which began in the late thirties, has continued to the present day. A world-wide assessment of educational activities in museums by UNESCO states that museums throughout the world are coming to regard themselves less as self-contained professional units than as cultural centers within their own communities (Hudson, 1977).

MUSEUMS AS EDUCATIONAL INSTITUTIONS

When contemporary museums present exhibitions to the public, they are expected to provide information about them. People want interpretation; they are curious, and they want to know what is important about the collections. It is in the best interest of the museum or historical site to nurture this inquisitiveness and develop it. Although museums have never presumed to offer total lifetime education, their resources have served to enrich and extend visitor knowledge and growth through contact with original artifacts and sites. Museum interpreters who are familiar with a variety of teaching strategies, and use them when interpreting the collections, can get messages across. Museum tours become credible when tour guides interpret collections meaningfully.

Museum education is a relatively new field of study. The philosophy, policies, and programs of any museum depend largely upon the priorities of the museum's administration and board. For various reasons, museum priorities are widely divergent, and educational practices are easily stifled. Museums, especially in America, depend upon private support and special public grant funds for their very existence. When financing is difficult, museums tend to cut staff, curtail collecting, and stop exhibit construction.

While museum educators believe education and interpretation are of fundamental importance, they will always have to share ideological space with that of curators for preserving and displaying collections, and with that of students, scholars, and collectors for research activities. Nonetheless, museums have assumed increasingly important educational roles for nearly fifty years. They provide not only guides but classes. And relatively recently they have added activities that instruct. We agree with those who say that one of the primary functions of museums today is to educate.

CONSERVE AND PROTECT

Conservation in the purest sense would mean locking objects into dustproof, dark, humidity-controlled rooms, never to expose them to the hazards of the environment. The best exhibitions require precious, often fragile objects to be moved about, sometimes for long distances. Each time a painting is moved, even within a museum, it suffers some wear, even if minute. Every visitor's shoes carry dust particles and bacteria that can create problems within carefully balanced atmospheres. This is particularly true of art objects. Often historic artifacts have suffered from the environment and daily wear long before they are acquired.

The case for conservation is well-founded, and it is one which interpreters should consider when planning educational projects or tours. It is the primary reason why museums substitute facsimiles for original objects in demonstrations, and why artifacts are seldom touched. Visitors will lose some of the excitement that comes from touching an original object, but dozens, perhaps hundreds, of hands touching irreplaceable surfaces can cause real harm. True conservation must be balanced with reason and sensible precautions.

Although there is ongoing discussion about the advisability of sending exhibitions to locations around the world, the objectives of exhibit travel are gaining an edge over those of conservation. A consensus is growing among museum administrators that traveling exhibits offer important educational opportunities. In other words, people want to learn about other places, times, and cultures, and the most informative way is to experience aspects of those cultures directly through their artifacts. The attendance figures for such "blockbuster" exhibitions as the King Tutankhamen, the Great Bronze Age of China, or the Vatican Exhibition prove that the public perceives in them inherent educational and cultural values, which contribute in significant ways to the life of the community.

MUSEUMS AND CHILDREN

Museum education for children is practiced all over the world, although each country emphasizes it differently. The most widely used "program" in museums is the guided tour. However, many visitors continue to walk through museums looking at collections on their own. Children are often encouraged to "explore" a museum and wander about without supervision.

Museums more recently have included participatory activities for visitors in addition to guided tours, encouraging discovery learning at the individual's own pace and level of interest (Marcouse, 1973). Moving exhibits, talking telephones, large to-scale models and real objects that can be entered (submarines and coal mines), audio-visual guides, activities that invite the visitor to touch, experiment, smell, hear and see the remarkable, the unusual, and the rare—are all worthwhile, dynamic, exciting education projects.

Museum educators world-wide emphasize participation and interaction with student visitors. The most widely used tour in Great Britain, for example, is a carefully orchestrated "discovery" method, planned in advance with schools. Further, multicultural education is emphasized in order to give students a view of world society. Museum educators in the Soviet Union are well-represented on the staff of most museums and provide excellent tours. Many museums in Mexico have "orientation rooms," which hold carefully selected objects and, perhaps, offer a film or slide show. Some museums have learning environments where students can do practical work which relates to an exhibit. Sometimes they can conduct actual experiments. History museums in the United States have areas where children can experience the past by using early tools or equipment, or can put on clothing styled in the period of the exhibit. Some science and children's museums display only interactive exhibits.

MUSEUMS AND SCHOOLS

Museums and schools are complementary. Museums can offer real objects—tangible examples of ideas, processes, natural environments, and history. Classroom experiences are limited to books, lectures, media, and simple hands-on experiences. The two institutions, by working together, can provide truly outstanding educational opportunities for young people. Teaching directly from original objects in a museum can enrich school learning, for interpretation can include new experiences in perceiving the objects.

However, the museum-school partnership is still not firmly established, as there are many problems. Relationships between museums and schools are still tentative and confused. This is unfortunate, considering that large numbers of school children are the main recipients of museum services. The number of art centers, museums, and historical sites which have established ongoing partnerships with schools are minuscule in number. Educators in both museums and schools are developing the resolve to promote strong and meaningful relations, and we may hope that workable policy and mutual dependency will emerge through persistent efforts.

Tour problems can arise. Many school tours lack specific learning objectives because of either lack of planning or previsit interaction with the schools. Some school groups are present for little more than an hour; moreover, they rarely return in the same year. In addition, large groups create difficulties for interpreters in their attempts to communicate with them.

The small museum can serve schools best by offering tours based on three or four topics which relate to specific school subjects. Tours that relate to "nothing" are soon forgotten. Such tours may be pleasing to adults, but unless they are relevant, these tours are wasted on students. A guide's ideas combined with a teacher's suggestions are likely to produce a tour that will assume importance in the eyes of students.

INTERPRETATION

Museum lectures and tours until the 1950s followed a conventional educational pattern: the instructor presented information, and the students listened, memorized it, and gave it back. It was a practice that had been established years earlier in schools where the teacher was assumed to be the fount of all knowledge. Through greater understanding of children's intellectual growth, schools have begun, in more recent years, to educate in more interactive ways. Museums have responded in similar fashion to these new insights about human growth and development.

Interpretation occurs in many forms. Maximum museum interpretation offers variation in information, visual and verbal, at many levels of understanding for many different audiences. Although much interpretation today is oral, many historic sites and museums in the past relied only on labels for interpretation. This minimal, one-directional technique, which ignores the interests of visitors and their backgrounds, requires that label information be on a level that most people are able to comprehend. Interpretation via labels is a difficult task, but museum visitor research is beginning to provide insights that are making label information and exhibit design more useful.

However, the best interpretation involves more than labels. It encompasses ongoing interaction between guides and visitors. Freeman Tilden, in **Interpreting Our Heritage** (1967), feels that the experiences visitors bring with them are the key to real interpretation, and he insists that tour information relate to it. Others feel that visitors' self-esteem is involved and that good interpretation must also respond to the personal idiosyncrasies of the members of each group. This challenge requires considerable tour guide sensitivity to particular circumstances.

THE INTERPRETER

The first docent program was begun by Benjamin Ives Gilman at the Museum of Fine Arts in Boston. In 1907 his gallery instruction program used "teacher-lecturers" to help "educate" people and to "elevate their lives," as discussed earlier in this chapter. Public instruction was free. It was provided by trained docents. Other museums soon adopted the idea, though art museums were the most enthusiastic in training the new docents. Volunteer lecturers appeared in major European museums at the turn of the century as well. By the early 1940s, museums were beginning to realize that tour guides had to be specialists in the subject matter of their museums. Tour guides were encouraged to use objects in teaching, but not to lecture. By 1971, art museum volunteers represented 67% of art museum workers (Newsom and Silver, 1978). Today, all types of museums are finding the volunteer work force indispensable for their programs. American museums have become dependent upon volunteer assistance in all areas of collecting, conserving, exhibiting and educating.

As schools increasingly use museums to help meet curriculum objectives, museums will not be able to provide the tours, workshops, and outreach projects without a volunteer staff. Many institutions use only volunteers as interpreters, and they become the sole "educators" for them.

THE FUTURE OF MUSEUM EDUCATION

Educational priorities change with regularity in museums, historical sites, and national parks, as we have seen over the past few generations. Yesterday's museums were, for the most part, empty of people. Today's museums have moved from the preservation of collections to teaching actively about them. Thousands of school classes a year are guided in museums. Life, as it was in past years, can be observed at Old Sturbridge Village, Williamsburg, and other historic sites. Citizens are more aware of cultural diversity because of more leisure time and frequent, extensive travel. The public clamors to see prominent exhibits. The history and culture of the world is more available through museums than through any other cultural institution.

Museums are making real attempts today to learn about their audiences and to respond to their preferences for exhibitions and education. People are more knowledgeable about their heritage, and they are becoming collectors themselves. "People's homes are becoming personal museums supplementing the external experience. Though subject to the tastes and economic capabilities of each individual . . . more 'education' and more museum-relevant expectations arise from this personal domain than any other" (Graburn, 1977, p. 7).

Changes in lifestyle and demands on museums may be greater in the years ahead than have been experienced in the past one hundred and fifty years. Mary Ellen Munley, in a study for the American Association of Museum's Commission on Museums for a New Century (1982) suggests that future populations may be vastly different. By 1990, 50% of the work force will be between the ages of 30 and 45, and the average population in the United States will be older. The minority population is increasing; Hispanics are the fastest growing group in the United States. More and more adults are and will be seeking adult education. Museums and other institutions must respond to this multiplicity of ages and cultures by presenting significant exhibits and interpreting their collections so that they will be understood by our multiethnic society.

In a major report prepared for the American Association of Museums, which examines issues facing museums today, the Commission on Museums for a New Century investigated the role of the museum regarding its obligations and responsibilities to society. The Commission affirms the traditional function of museums while highlighting education as a priority. Ellen Cochran Hicks, Commission Project Director, in discussing the report, said that "museums are our collective memory, our chronicle of human creativity, our window on the natural world. To change these basic functions would be to alter the way people are able to perceive the continuity of their existence" (Hicks, 1983, p. 64). However, the Commission feels that while there are more educational programs, one aspect that has not been examined thoroughly, and which should be addressed, is how people learn in museums (Commission on Museums for a New Century, 1984). Museums not only preserve our culture, but they must assume the responsibility for passing it on to new generations by becoming centers of learning in their own right. In this context, museum interpreters, as spokespersons for museums and historic sites, become critical sources of educational information.

REFERENCES

Adam, T. R. (1939). **Museums and Popular Culture.** American Association for Adult Education. New York: George Grady Press.

Bay, A. I. (1984). Practicality in the light of perfection: museum education then and now. **Roundtable Reports: The Journal of Museum Education.** **9**(2,3), 3-5.

Booth, J. H., Krockover, G. H., Woods, P. R. (1982). **Creative Museum Methods and Educational Techniques.** Springfield, Illinois: Charles C. Thomas.

Commission on Museums for a New Century. (1984). **Museums for a New Century.** Washington, DC: American Association of Museums.

Gilman, B. I. (1918). **Museum Ideals of Purpose and Method.** Cambridge, Massachusetts: Riverside Press.

Graburn, N. H. H. (1977). The museum and the visitor experience. **The Visitor and The Museum.** Berkeley: Museum Educators of the American Association of Museums, Lowie Museum of Anthropology, University of California.

Hicks, E. C. (1983). In pursuit of the future. A report from the commission on museums for a new century. **Museum News. 61**(6), 61-65.

Hudson, K. (1977). **Museums for the 1980s: A Survey of World Trends.** Paris: UNESCO.

Marcouse, R. (1973). **Museums, Imagination and Education.** Paris: UNESCO.

Munley, M. E. (1982). Looking ahead. **Museum News. 61**(6), 66-69.

Newsom, B. Y., and Silver, A. Z. (Eds.). (1978). **The Art Museum as Educator.** Berkeley: University of California Press.

Richardson, E. (1963). The museum in america, 1963. Paper presented at the 1963 Annual Meeting of the American Association of Museums, Seattle, Washington. Printed in **Museum News, 62**(3), 41-45.

Silver, A. Z. (1978). Issues in art museum education. In B. Y. Newsom and A. Z. Silver (Eds.), **The Art Museum as Educator,** 13-20. Berkeley: University of California Press.

Tilden, F. (1967). **Interpreting Our Heritage** (rev. ed.). Nashville, Tennessee: American Association of State and Local History.

Tomkins, C. (1970). **Merchants and Masterpieces: The Story of the Metropolitan Museum of Art.** New York: E. P. Dutton.

Wertz, L. E. (1984). Designs on excellence: the 1984 American Association of Museums publication competition. **Museum News, 63**(2), 41-45.

Winstanley, B. R. (1967). **Children and Museums.** Oxford, England: Basil Blackwell and Mott, Ltd.

CHAPTER THREE
How People Learn

Overview • Learning Defined • Three Learning Domains • Two Basic Descriptions of Learning • John Dewey: Education, and Learning

OVERVIEW

How do theories of learning affect tour guides and their presentations? In many different ways. There are several approaches to learning, but only a few of them are useful to guides who lead tours or teach about a museum exhibit. As we consider how people learn in Chapter Three, our discussion will be based on the following five points. Each of them contributes to the broad perspective we must have if we are to understand the nature of learning in museum settings.

1. Learning is a change in human capability which is retained.

2. There are three domains of learning: the *cognitive* which deals with intellectual understanding; the *affective* which is centered on emotional levels of understanding; and the *motor,* which pertains to the acquisition of behavioral skills.

3. Of the three learning domains (cognitive, affective, and motor), cog-

nitive approaches are the most helpful in a museum-type setting, especially when those in affective and motor domains are used to supplement those in the cognitive domain. As children mature, they move from concrete to abstract thinking, that is, from specific thoughts to general concepts. Piaget's theory of cognitive development, which will be described in the pages ahead, is one of the more useful approaches to tour design, but it requires that docents/interpreters understand children's stages of cognitive development.

4. Learning interpersonal skills is affected by the quality of social interaction and the kinds of experiences a young person has had. The child, in addition to learning how to use logic and symbols, moves from an "egocentric" (self-centered) perspective of those around him toward a more objective, societal one.

5. Active involvement in learning tasks enhances interest, an important condition of learning. By incorporating one or more discovery techniques in tour plans, visitors will have increased opportunities to focus on the tour subject. (See Chapter Five).

LEARNING DEFINED

Today's museums, historical sites, and national parks strive to present tours that offer visitors stimulating and valuable learning experiences. However, how is learning to "happen" in the unique setting of the museum or historical site? This is a perplexing problem for the guide.

Learning theories are complex; nonspecialists have difficulty understanding them. They deal with capabilities at particular levels of development and comprehension. Learning theories are developed and researched in academia, gain or lose support in that setting, and then emerge in school environments and museum settings watered-down and barely usable. Discussions about them are usually available only in textbooks written for professional educators.Learning theories are, in fact, both contradictory and complementary. As Robert Gagne wrote in **The Conditions of Learning,**

> *I do not think learning is a phenomenon which can be explained by simple theories, despite the admitted intellectual appeal that such theories have. Although . . . [I] have tried for years to account for actual instances of learning in terms of a small number of principles, I am currently convinced that it cannot be done. The principles of learning that apply to education are dependent upon what kind of capability is being learned (Gagne, 1965, p. v).*

Nonetheless, as tour guides and interpreters, there are key principles that we can use in devising effective and rewarding tours. Our task as interpreters is to avoid a simplified, arbitrary view of how people learn.

Learning is a continuous process for everyone: we interpret our surroundings as we take in information through our senses. Learning takes place even before we learn to talk. We learn from what we observe and from what other people tell us. We learn as we play and as we practice the instructions of others. As we adapt biologically to our environment, we also adapt intellectually. We acquire knowledge as we experience the world through organized learning. Consider, then, a definition of learning that meets the needs of the docent/interpreter:

> *Learning is a change in human disposition or capability, which can be retained, and which is not simply ascribable to the process of growth. The kind of change called learning exhibits itself as a change in behavior . . . the change may be, and often is, an increased capability for some type of performance. It may also be an altered disposition of the sort called "attitude," or "interest," or "value" (Gagne, 1965, p. 5).*

THREE LEARNING DOMAINS

Whether we use abstract thought and concepts, exchange feelings with others, or operate mechanical equipment, some kind of learning is taking place. Learning theorists have grouped the kinds of learning that occur into three learning "domains" or categories, which they describe as **cognitive, affective,** and **motor** (or skill). The three domains constitute a hierarchy as defined by levels of comprehension or understanding.

THE COGNITIVE DOMAIN: Thinking and Understanding

When we are thinking, for example, about the history of the Hopis, the development of Impressionism, or the female role in Colonial America, we are working in the cognitive domain. Eliot Eisner, a distinguished learning theorist and art educator, interprets this domain to include "the process through which the organism becomes aware of the environment" (Eisner, 1981, p. 48). Awareness, as Eisner sees it, leads to a "reading" of one's surroundings. The challenge in the cognitive domain for museum visitors is to translate new information learned from exhibits into meaningful concepts and knowledge. This requires reasoning, interpretation, and synthesis. Tours for different age groups thus should be designed to correspond appropriately to their various levels of experience and understanding.

THE AFFECTIVE DOMAIN: Emotions or Feelings

At this level of learning, individuals center on the feeling or emotional level of learning. For example, when guides express their personal feelings or attitudes toward aspects of contemporary art or their sentiments toward preservation of an endangered species, they are offering learning experiences in the affective domain. When visitors are asked to express their own feelings about an exhibit or object, they are reacting in the affective domain. Feelings of passion, indignation, fear, anger, and so forth can be aroused in cognitive discussion. Sometimes, therefore, a written interpretation or description of an exhibit which was designed for cognitive learning may also influence affective learning.

THE MOTOR OR SKILL DOMAIN: Learning and Carrying out Physical Tasks

People acquire the skills to carry out coordinated, physical-level tasks in the context of this learning domain. For example, when visitors are expected to proceed through an exhibit in a prescribed manner, operate a computer, or push a button, the first level of comprehension is simply that of figuring out what the necessary steps should be. Skill learning, particularly for children, may be an important first step in certain kinds of interpretation and a prerequisite to cognitive learning.

The design of an effective tour or workshop should begin with consideration of the three learning domains. The activity will be more effective in attaining its objectives when learning is planned in the context of the appropriate domain. Though this sounds complicated, common sense and reference to the definitions should easily dictate the proper strategy. Examples: (1) Lectures are usually given to increase visitors' knowledge; therefore, they are in the cognitive domain. A lecture-style tour will allow for the efficient communication of information but it will seldom change feelings and emotions or lead to skill development. (2) In contrast, a docent is occasionally confronted with a specific objective to change attitudes and feelings. A lecture designed to include many facts will be less effective for this purpose than an open discussion about visitors' impressions. However, when feelings are discussed, attitudes may change while knowledge may increase very little. (3) Since all kinds of performance skills belong in the motor domain, they are taught more effectively through participatory activities or practice sessions. Growth in cognitive knowledge and change in attitudes may occur as a by-product when skill learning is the focus of the activity.

Since tours and lectures usually communicate information about an exhibit, the content of most tours corresponds to the **cognitive** domain. Occasionally, especially with children, an interpreter may include affective expressions or teach a specific motor skill to help visitors understand a point. As an example of how all three domains might be interpreted, consider a history museum interpreter, taking a group of fifth graders through a restored Victorian-era house:

(Cognitive Domain) "The man who built this house was a merchant. When he was finished, the house was the most modern in town, but it had no electricity. How do you think they lighted the house in the evening?"

(Cognitive Domain) "When electricity was finally installed, what other objects could the family purchase for the house?"

(Affective Domain) "If you could walk into the kitchen on Thanksgiving morning, how do you think the house would smell? Would you be excited? What foods might be prepared—can you imagine the turkey or onions cooking?"

(Motor Domain) "Take a turn pumping water into the sink, grinding wheat, stirring batter, or churning butter."

TWO BASIC DESCRIPTIONS OF LEARNING

The two basic theories of learning described here were developed in the "stimulus-response" and the "cognitive" schools of psychology. Although museum interpretation is concerned primarily with the latter, docents should become acquainted with the S-R theory, because it demonstrates, from another perspective, how people learn.

THE STIMULUS-RESPONSE SCHOOL

This position evolved from the work of Ivan Pavlov (1849-1936), an early Russian psychologist, Edward L. Thorndike (1874-1949), an American psychologist, and B. F. Skinner, (1904–), a contemporary American psychologist. Generally, this theory suggests that **learning evolves out of the development of associations between stimuli and responses.** It implies that learning can be programmed—that instructors can take control of the learner's environment. Persons learn to respond correctly to all sorts of stimuli—whether hunger pangs, classwork, or an interpreter's questions. A response is said to be correct if the teacher, parent, or tour guide "reinforces" it, that is, informs the learner by praise or some other "reward" that it is the correct response. Such events occur hundreds of times a day for all of us and they are said to shape our behavior. People who draw upon this theory believe strongly that reinforcement can produce learning and change behavior. It is an especially popular procedure among those who advocate programmed computer instruction and rigidly controlled classroom teaching. While the S-R school has made an invaluable contribution to psychology and to the developing "information processing" field, there are few psychologists today who strictly adhere to this position as the sole explanation for learning. It is important for anyone who deals with learners, nonetheless, to be familiar with the theory because sometimes learning situations can be approached from this perspective. Museum experiences involving motor skills or demonstration exhibits are particularly relevant, i.e., scratching minerals for hardness, or identifying leaves by matching shapes.

THE COGNITIVE SCHOOL

There are many cognitive theories of learning; all of them, however, are concerned with the intellectual processes that affect behavior. Cognition deals with thinking, reasoning, and ways of obtaining knowledge. Learning is thought of as more than associations between stimuli and responses. **Reasoning involves the development of symbolic images of reality and the use of these mental images.** Reasoning stimulates a search for relationships and solutions from what is already known; familiar elements are combined in different ways to create novel or original answers. Knowledge is the result of the rearrangement of ideas and experiences into concepts.

Concept formation, which begins in childhood, involves categorizing information. When we discover how different things in the environment share features (commonness), we identify this similarity by saying that we have abstracted a generalization or rule. Consider:

Experience: A child burns its hand when touching a pan on the stove.
Concept: The pan is "hot" because it is on a fire.
Generalization or rule: Objects get "hot" when in a pan on a hot stove. "Hot" objects burn, burns cause pain.

Experience: A child learns that a ball is "round," a circle is "round," joining hands in a circle is walking "a-round," and so on.
Concept: "Round" is the name of a class of objects (Gagne, 1965, p. 183).
Generalization or rule: Things having a circular shape are "round."

The illustrations indicate how we find or conceptualize the essential bases for shared features. Abstract reasoning, as illustrated above, always involves complex relationships among concepts. As we grow older, mature thought produces a hierarchy, or structure of concepts, in which concepts build from the concrete to the abstract, one upon the other, until a high level of understanding is attained. Consider the following ascending levels of abstractness: (1) quarter, (2) coin, (3) currency, or (1) the "Mona Lisa," (2) painting, (3) art. In the latter instance, the "Mona Lisa" is (1) a famous painting hanging in the Louvre. At the next level, there are many works including the Mona Lisa that can be called (2) "paintings." Finally, the abstract concept (3) "art" embraces countless objects including, for example, sculpture, weaving, and photography, all of which share such qualities as cultural value, recognition, uniqueness, beauty, workmanship, and so forth. Therefore, the hierarchy progresses from the concrete "Mona Lisa" to the abstract concept of "art." One of the primary instructional goals of tour guides and interpreters is to discuss and teach concepts. Teaching effectiveness will depend upon presenting suitable concepts to the visitor at appropriate levels of abstraction.

Cognitive learning is the most important theory of the two discussed here for tour guides. The following discussion, therefore, analyzes two distinct aspects of cognitive learning:

1. Cognitive Development—how children develop intellectually and move toward maturity.
2. Information Processing—how people assimilate information and experiences and how they develop new concepts and acquire knowledge.

COGNITIVE DEVELOPMENT

Jean Piaget (1896-1980) is foremost among psychologists who have analyzed the development of logical reasoning from childhood to adolescence. After his book, **Language and Thought of the Child,** appeared in 1923, he and his collaborators published over a period of a half-century more than thirty books and hundreds of research studies. Piaget's most important contribution was to describe the steps that young people go through in developing the capacity to reason and learn. His theory explains how children function intellectually in terms of their own "knowing." Cognitive growth, or the capacity to reason logically and learn, occurs when young people recognize that they are coping inadequately with the environment. Both physical and mental actions become better coordinated, and new patterns of thought are constructed as the growing child struggles to find more effective relationships among perplexing aspects of reality. Infants are born with only a few reflexes, but immediately, they begin to absorb new information. As Piaget said, "to know an object is to act upon it" (Piaget, 1964).

Children are thus stimulated developmentally by the world around them to manipulate their environment—to sense, touch, order, count, compare and contrast, abstract and generalize. They learn from successes and failures in solving problems. Since Piagetian theory suggests that cognitive development occurs in a context of inquiry, many educators have applied it to a subsidiary theory known as "discovery learning." Discovery learning is child-centered and emphasizes active participation in learning activities. Ideas about discovery learning were developed earlier; now Piaget's views provide them with theoretical structure (See Chapter Five).

Piaget believed that children think and reason differently as they move through stages of cognitive or intellectual development. According to the theory, each stage describes a particular form of cognition. The first stage of cognitive development indicates that physical movements and sensations generate the earliest signs of intellect; the second, that mental representations are beginning to influence how the child adapts; the third, that impressions from concrete experiences produce simple forms of abstract reasoning; the fourth, which usually coincides with adolescence, that capacity to deal with abstract relationships and inferential reasoning enables individuals to follow the form of a logical discussion. Piaget's notion of progression implies that growth in logical capability emerges in about the same order in all children. Elementary reasoning becomes integral to later, more complex reasoning, and young people of roughly the same age solve all sorts of tasks and problems in similar ways.

Children, adolescents, and adults will consider a museum exhibit according to their particular views of the world. How they understand a tour, workshop or lecture-discussion on art, science, history, and so on, will depend upon their level of cognitive maturity. The following list of Piaget's stages, and the ages to which they roughly correspond, is presented to illustrate the different cognitive levels at which tour guides and interpreters might present concepts to young people.

THE FOUR STAGES OF COGNITIVE DEVELOPMENT—PIAGET

Stage One: Sensorimotor
Age Range: infancy to about two years
Characteristics: Infants begin to learn about the world around them; they acquire knowledge by movements and actions. External stimulation evokes responses directly, so infants are dominated by perceptions. At about ten months, however, infants reach the cognitive milestone of **object permanence.** They realize that objects do not go out of existence when they go out of sight. (For example, infants learn that parents will reappear while playing peek-a-boo.)

Stage Two: Symbolic, Pre-Logical
Age Range: two years to about seven years (preschool to second grade)
Characteristics: A major turning point in intellectual development occurs at about two years of age when behavior begins to follow symbolic processes. Language capability is now emerging, and children are beginning to respond to events, not reflexively, but after thinking about them. Nevertheless, children's reasoning continues to be dominated by perceptions and what seems to be rather than what they know ought to be. Since children do not understand causal relationships, events that happen together are simply assumed to be causally related. A child may think that all the baby birds in a mother hen's flock belong to that hen, although one of them happens to be a baby duck. Explanations are drawn largely from sensory experiences; thus, children are likely to focus on obvious details of size, color, or familiarity and neglect other important but less apparent ones. Children at this stage do not plan activities. They move from one thing or event rather randomly; one exhibit or picture will have no relationship to the next. The world for them is one of "pictures" and "images."

Stage Three: Operational (logical-concrete)
Age Range: seven years to eleven years (third grade to seventh grade)
Characteristics: Piaget describes cognitive behavior during this time as **concrete** because, although ability to deal with simple logical relationships is emerging, reasoning is still dominated by direct personal experience. Relationships among objects are based on features of obvious similarity (size, color, or shape), while more obscure relationships, which may possibly be more important, are overlooked. (Dinosaurs are related on the bases of their hugeness; at this time it is not important to the child to distinguish between those which were plant-eating and those which were meat-eating.) During this period children begin to reflect upon relationships and apply reasoning to them. They can correct errors as they attempt to gain perspective. A transformation in reasoning processes now occurs (Piaget describes it as conservation.) It enables children to "hold" in their minds the basic identity of objects or situations despite external changes in them. They recognize grandfather even though he is disguised in a Santa Claus suit, or that an apple is still an apple even though its appearance changes after baking. Children thereby can maintain a stable perspective toward important aspects of a situation, even though they are considering it from various perspectives. The mental operations associated with this period thus enable children to "play" with all sorts of categories and groupings of mental images, which brings them to the threshold of true logical reasoning.

Stage Four: Mature Thought (Formal Operations)
Age Range: early adolescence through adulthood, (from about the eighth grade onward)
Characteristics: The major turning point in cognitive development occurs when young people begin to see, in hypothetical terms, the probable causes of relationships. ("How might it be if . . .") They acquire the capacity to analyze connections between premises and conclusions and to infer with some assurance which of the connections or relationships has the greater probability of being true. Although initial theorizing may be incomplete and first efforts at reflection may be awkward, ahead is a world that is both systematic and comprehensive. Adolescents acquire the intellectual potential to put it all together. Whatever the context—physics, economics, politics, or art—"formal operations" (inferring cause and effect, imagining or hypothesizing, drawing conclusions, etc.) are applicable. However, adolescents and adults do not apply logical analysis in every practical real-life setting. There are two reasons why. First, application of formal operations presumes that experience with the subject matter has been sufficiently meaningful to enable the individual to organize it conceptually. A young person who, for some reason, forms negative or incorrect concepts of modern art or frontier life, for example, will be unable to develop useful information from experiences in these contexts without

additional exposure and information. Also, possession of the logical skills to reason hypothetically about possibilities will lead nowhere when facts are incomprehensible. Second, analytic skills seldom are flawless. The overall experiences of growing up bring about enormous individual differences among adolescents in their reasoning powers.

IMPLICATIONS OF PIAGET'S THEORY FOR INTERPRETERS AND MUSEUM EDUCATORS

Although Piaget developed a hierarchy of stages, or sequence of steps in cognitive (intellectual) development, through which all children are said to pass, the stages are not fixed rigidly at specific ages. Tour guides should not assume that all children at age six, nine, or any given age, will be alike in their cognitive reasoning. Piaget's cognitive theory, nonetheless, is especially relevant in the context of tour education. **It clarifies how concepts are developed from simple to complex, or from concrete to abstract.** It indicates how children progress in organizing and assimilating knowledge about the world around them. Since museums deal primarily with ideas, knowledge, and transfer of information, educators can draw upon understanding of Piaget's stages of cognitive development to plan both museum and school tours at appropriate levels of comprehension for their audiences.

For example, Piaget's theory shows how instruction and teaching must fit into ways children think and reason. Interpreters must guard against meaningless verbalizations—"this is beautiful" or "highly valued" or "shows exquisite workmanship;" abstract thinking is virtually impossible for younger children and very difficult for adolescents when the subject matter is strange to them. If a tour is given in a haphazard, unfocused manner, children will only understand a small part of the tour, or be totally lost, and adolescents will lose interest quickly when comprehension becomes too great a struggle. Both children and adolescents easily process new information incorrectly. They may reject it or become interested in something else irrelevant to the discussion, but understandable to them. They may be distracted, too, by class misbehavior or another exhibit.

Although children and adolescents vary a great deal in their levels of reasoning, Piaget's theory provides broad guidelines for determining where to begin teaching and touring. **Understanding the cognitive capabilities of young people and adults at different stages of reasoning provides the interpreter with bases for preparing presentations for given age levels.**

INFORMATION PROCESSING

Information processing describes the ways we store, use, and retrieve information in our memories. Piaget contributed to the identification of stages in the development of logical reasoning and understanding; other psychologists have looked more precisely at information assimilation and use.

Social Cognition as an Aspect of Information Processing. Information processing theorists have turned recently to the study of ways interpersonal interactions influence cognitive behavior. This new field of investigation is known as social cognition. "Social cognition can be defined as how people think about other people and about themselves, or how people come to know their social world" (Muuss, 1982, p. 232). Beginning in the mid 1960s, psychologists began studying how people "perceive" their world and how social development parallels that of cognitive (intellectual) development. Their research shows that children and adolescents begin to make social inferences—to infer the intentions of others—in accordance with the development of their cognitive skills. Children and adolescents, that is, use their cognitive (intellectual) competencies in social situations, just as in analyzing the physical world, to understand and predict how another person may feel or behave.

In learning to understand other persons, children and adolescents begin to think about their thoughts, intentions, and emotions. They ask "how will they behave?" Perceiving information about the social world (and the physical world) is acquired through observation, trial and error activity, and discovery. In the maturing process, thinking is focused first on physical, then on social, and finally, on moral dimensions. Children become more and more skillful in separating their viewpoints from those of others, and they become more adept at perceiving correctly how others are thinking. Robert Selman (Muuss, 1982) has categorized how children understand the people around them—in their social world—in terms of five role-taking stages. At increasing levels of understanding, children think about people as individuals and about relationships between people (as indicated by their interpretations of friendship, hostility, customary and unusual behavior, etc.). Selman's five stages are described briefly below.

1. Age 3 to 6: Egocentric perspective

   Children are concerned with their own ideas and perspectives. They cannot understand that their own perception may not be the correct one, and that there may be different points of view.

2. Age 5 to 9: Subjective perspective

   Children begin to realize that others can have different perspectives from their own. Judgements about others are derived on the basis of physical observations; children know that others may interpret the same social situation differently, but except for gross assumptions

TABLE ONE

PIAGET'S STAGES OF COGNITIVE DEVELOPMENT
SELMAN'S STAGES OF SOCIAL COGNITION

AGE	PIAGET CATEGORIES	PIAGET CHARACTERISTICS	AGE	SELMAN CATEGORIES	SELMAN CHARACTERISTICS
Infancy–2	Sensorimotor	1. Not applicable	**None**	None	None
Age: 2–7	Pre-logical	1. Explores symbols 2. Language begins 3. Accepts what seems to be 4. Does not understand causal relationships	**Age: 3–6**	Egocentric	1. Individual Concepts 2. Cannot differentiate between self and other perspective
			Age: 5–9	Subjective Perspective-taking	1. Friendships 2. Judgement based on physical observation 3. Another person can have different perspective
Age: 7–11	Concrete Operations	1. Involved with the present & concrete 2. Begins inductive reasoning; cause & effect 3. Begins to put objects in some kind of order	**Age: 7–12**	Self-Reflective Thinking	1. Peer-group concepts 2. Can make inferences about other people's perspective
			Age: 10–15	Mutual Perspective-taking	1. Parent-child concepts (better understanding of relationship) 2. Can move to neutral third person perspective 3. Can conceptualize to general social system
Age: Adolescent to adult	Formal Operations	1. Can use logic effectively 2. Can think in abstract terms with words & symbols 3. Can think in past and future as well as present 4. Inductive, deductive hypothetical thinking	**Age: Adolescent to adult**	In-depth and societal perspective	1. Societal perspective 2. Understands each person has own system of analysis

about why others act as they do, they are unable to determine what the perspectives of others may be.

3. Age 7 to 12: Self-reflective thinking perspective

Children can understand another person's perspective, can make inferences about the perspectives of other people, and can think subjectively about their own behavior. They become aware that other people have different values, feelings, and thoughts.

4. Age 10 to 15 (early adolescence): Mutual perspective

Adolescents can move beyond their own and another person's perspective to that of a neutral third person. They can also generalize concepts to the larger social system.

5. Age 16 to adulthood: In-depth and societal perspective-taking.

Coordination of third-person perspectives—a societal view emerges. Social facts are understood as being interpreted by other individuals according to their own systems of analysis, that is, their own unique perspective.

As Selman's outline indicates, early in social cognitive development, children (to about seven or eight years of age) attribute their own thoughts and attitudes to others. As another psychologist, J. H. Flavell, suggests, children at this age are likely, too, to confuse the perceptions of others with their own. It is a problem of "perceptual role taking," of being unaware of another's visual perspective. For example, children who are on the opposite side of a sculpture from an interpreter will perceive the sculpture as they actually see it; they will be unaware that the guide and other members of the group have different perceptions because they are looking at it from other angles. Younger children assume that the guide sees the sculpture from a perspective similar to their own—from only that one angle. If the docent's interpretation of the object doesn't fit the child's perspective, it probably will be rejected. Similarly, young children will draw a head in profile with the eye depicted on the side of the head as if viewed from the front, as in the Early Egyptian manner. Thus, in both instances, children are unable to separate what they know or have learned from what they think that they see.

The emotional content of subject matter discussed in a tour is understood best when it has been experienced. Although children may not yet be at the level of abstract thinking, they are able to understand simple, "appropriate" emotions. Anger, happiness, or indignation in a sculpture or painting may be seen as appropriate because these emotions have occurred in the realm of children's experience. On the other hand, emotions are least understood when they seem inappropriate (Iannotti, 1978). Sometimes, however, it is necessary to talk about complex objects from the more narrow perspective of visual form or appearance. Works of art that have complex or conflicting meaning, which may require many levels of comprehension, may be totally beyond the understanding of children younger than about twelve years. The fact that abstract contemporary art is so difficult for children to understand is a major reason why they may dislike it. The only meaning that they can draw from such art is what they can associate to their own reality.

The ways children or young people think about others thus affect how they relate to the guide and other members of the tour, and how they conceptualize information presented to them on the tour. By using Piaget's stages of intellectual development and Selman's social development levels (See Table 1), interpreters can be more effective in designing tours; they will know how young people deal with symbols and logic, and they will understand their levels of interpersonal understanding. Interpreters should plan tours from the point of view of both the intellectual capability and the social maturity of children. **Cognitive ability and social cognitive awareness are equally important.**

> *The educational method that appears to be particularly valuable in stimulating interpersonal growth is not a lecture or expository mode of teaching, but an exploratory mode of teaching, such as discussion and debate (Muuss, 1982, p. 252).*

The docent must be concerned with the perspectives of the child, young person, or adult, know how they understand the feelings, thoughts, and behavior of others, and understand how this perspective will influence realization of the learning objectives of the tour.

Learning by Discovery. Learning by discovery is a technique of learning that stimulates cognitive activity by involving persons in several domains of learning at the same time. Different theorists have focused on different aspects: what teachers must do, what learners do when they learn by discovery, and the end product. It has been called an "experience" as well as a teaching strategy. Many psychologists believe that this approach is a very effective way to learn, and supporters range from those who believe in unorganized, random learning to those who advocate structured and preplanned discovery. As an example of the "random" approach, Bruno Bettleheim, in an address at the 1979 "Children in Museums" conference at the Smithsonian, urged that there be "no educational programs" and that children should be allowed to wander on their own as he did as a child (cited in Lehman & Igoe, 1981, p. 18). "Discovery" in this context is wholly unstructured.

Learning by discovery, which involves preplanning, however, is probably one of the best teaching approaches in the museum setting. This is because of the nature of the institution, that is, to relate the characteristics of objects to one another, and to promote general principles underlying historical contexts, environmental effects, media, and artistic intentions. As noted earlier, the discovery of generalizations, or the formation of concepts, is (1) a process of search and (2) a process of selection (Gagne, 1966, p. 135).

Jerome Bruner believes that discovery is the main process which accounts for learning. Humankind, he says, learns through insights, by rearranging or changing previous ideas, perceptions, and experiences which lead to new thought patterns. Therefore, in contrast to Bettleheim's "wandering," Bruner would structure the environment and set up ways to prepare pupils for discovery. His approach would include defining strategies, selecting information, using cues, and cultivating motives. For example, guides, in setting up tours according to Bruner's suggestions, would establish objectives, furnish the route and tour "pauses" at specific locations in order for visitors to address the objectives. Tour members would "discover" the content, but the content would be preselected to ensure that the learning experiences supported the objectives.

Professor Robert Glaser, in addition to structuring the environment, would specify performance standards, guide visitors from one "phase" to another, and evaluate whether they attained competence relative to teaching and learning objectives (cited in Klausmeier, 1979). Glaser's suggestions are particularly relevant for school environments where evaluational activities are more common and practical than in museums. Nonetheless, museum educators and teachers might collaborate in setting learning objectives and in planning evaluations to ensure that school tours based on discovery methods are effective.

Glaser's viewpoint also suggests that visitors be exposed to many kinds of stimulation to help them become "visually and aurally sensitive." They would then become more aware of details and of similarities and differences between objects. For example, visitors can use their senses by feeling bins of seeds or nails, smelling paint or bread, or listening to sounds generated by the environment and other people. The point is that individuals are able to learn classifications and generalizations both much earlier (when age is a factor) and more effectively when the world is experienced through the senses as well as represented symbolically (Klausmeier, 1979). This is most easily practiced at living history museums. A multisensory tour helps visitors generalize about objects in an exhibit and discriminate between things that do not fit into the same "class." People thus may more easily comprehend common links between objects. They begin to understand important concepts underlying an exhibit when they have a heightened awareness of all the clues that will help them understand it.

One advantage of learning by discovery is that the tour experience is nonthreatening. Fear of mistakes or getting wrong answers are reduced, thus assuring a more pleasurable experience, particularly for the young. In discovery, "the concept of error may become quite meaningless. The consequences of different courses of action are rendered equivalent, as in a setting where all behaviors are equally rewarded or unrewarded. The error concept is irrelevant when the goal is exploration" (Shulman & Keislar, 1966, p. 96). More involvement is demanded of visitors, which leads to greater attention to the information being presented. Visitors are more interested and stimulated. A key goal in encouraging learning is that new concepts will be understood and learned when differences and similarities among existing concepts become clear (Shulman & Keislar, 1966).

The effectiveness of discovery learning is dependent on individual abilities, interests, and cognitive levels of reasoning. Visitors to a museum sort their experiences, or "arrange" learning opportunities for themselves to fit their needs. Learning by discovery will occur on the multiple levels of cognitive, affective, and skill learning. Although it is guided primarily by the learner, it is interactive instruction. Tour guides do not simply withhold answers from visitors. One major problem is that it is difficult to anticipate with certainty what persons will do in the discovery situation. Clearly, it works best when tour guides try to anticipate how visitors will respond and ensure that sources of information are available to them.

Museums should be responsible for more than merely transferring information by means of supplying facts and showing examples of a culture or an artist's work. Helping people grow, and providing greater meaning to them, requires allowing them to match their "cognitive structures" with information about the objects and exhibits.

JOHN DEWEY: EDUCATION AND LEARNING

John Dewey exerted tremendous influence upon American education from about the turn of the century until the 1940s. He espoused learning by doing and experiencing—having "quality" experiences. He was concerned that experiences not be separated from one another, as he believed that all experiences stay in memory and "connect" with other experiences to make things meaningful. Dewey believed that, in the schools of his day, facts and information were removed from their proper setting in life's experience and that general principles about them were being applied in isolation. In an attempt to bring the "proper setting" into the classroom, schools adopted such "doing" experiences as carpentry, painting, spinning, etc. However, it is generally thought by today's educators that offering such activities do not enhance cognitive learning. "Hands-on" classroom projects often present experiences unrelated to concepts important to meaningful learning. A child cannot learn about pioneer life by simply spinning or riding in a buckboard; nor can a child understand folk art or creativity by coloring, working with clay, or building a birdhouse. However, even today, there are art, science, and history educational programs in museums which mimic the discredited school programs of those early days. These programs are mere caricatures of John Dewey's child-centered approach.

Many museums currently present activity-oriented tours and workshops which are intended to teach exhibit-related facts and principles, yet which fail to stretch visitors' imaginative and reasoning powers. Experience-oriented activities which are separated from the content of the exhibit or collection will not produce effective learning.

Organized museum learning requires that learning objectives be set and that tour guides know how to communicate them, understand how visitors are likely to respond to questions and information, and reinforce appropriate answers. Tour guides must ensure that learning occurs at proper cognitive, affective, and skill levels of comprehension. The tour will be most successful in bringing about the highest levels of cognitive learning when exhibit information encourages involvement, interaction, and reasoning.

For learning to really hold or last, the interpreter must bridge the gap between concepts and relationships associated with the collections and the personal experiences and capacity for learning of visitors. The interpreter should keep in mind that wholly disconnected or unrelated experiences in the museum may cause pleasurable feelings, but such experiences are also often meaningless.

REFERENCES

Eisner, E. W. (1981). The role of the arts in cognition and curriculum. **Phi Delta Kappan, 63**(1), 48-52.

Gagne, R. M. (1965). **The Conditions of Learning.** New York: Holt, Rinehart and Winston, Inc.

Gagne, R. M. (1966). Varieties of learning and the concept of discovery. In L. S. Shulman and E. R. Keislar (Eds.) **Learning by Discovery: A Critical Appraisal,** 135-150. Chicago: Rand McNally.

Ianotti, R. J. (1978). Effect of role-taking experiences on role-taking, empathy, altruism, and aggression. **Developmental Psychology, 14,** 119-124.

Klausmeier & Associates. (1979). **Cognitive Learning & Development: Information Processing and Piagetian Perspective.** Cambridge, Massachusetts: Ballinger

Lehman, S. N., & Igoe, K. (Eds.). (1981). **Museum School Partnerships.** Washington, DC: George Washington University.

Muuss, R. E. (1982). **Theories of Adolescence.** New York: Random House.

Piaget, J. (1964). Development and Learning. **Journal of Research in Science Teaching,** 3, 176-186. New York: Wiley & Sons.

Shulman, L. S., & Keislar, E. (Eds.). (1966). **Learning by Discovery: A Critical Appraisal.** Chicago: Rand McNally.

CHAPTER FOUR
Museums and Learning

The Museum Experience • Stimulation for Learning • Learning Environments • Learning Structures • The Learning Focus • Learning Methods For Tours

THE MUSEUM EXPERIENCE

Learning in museums can be unique, for a single museum experience may include several ways of learning, i.e., cognitive, affective, and motor learning. Teaching, or interpreting exhibits in museums, can be approached differently from that of classroom teaching. Each museum possesses potential for learning through its exhibits, written materials, working models, and supplemental information. Tour guides have a variety of options for visitor learning available to them and they can be highly responsive to individual differences. Of course, how objects are displayed and how information is shared will vary from museum to museum. Some museums will offer visitors a range of learning encounters; others will encourage them to learn primarily at their own pace and to select from written sources of information provided by their staffs.

One major difficulty with the self-guided approach is that visitors are inclined to seek out specific experiences and objects which are personally meaningful to them. Such experiences may only reinforce what they already know. When museum learning becomes self-selected, visitors are not likely to expand their knowledge significantly.

Volunteer guides are able especially to supplement and extend information provided on exhibit labels and signs. Tour guides have the advantage of being able to learn about visitor characteristics before a tour, and they can use this information, both during preparation and during the actual tour. They can take into consideration all the factors associated with the museum experience: the environment, the stimulation of the objects, a variety of possible ways of learning, and the focusing power of a learning objective.

Direct interaction with original artifacts is one of the more exciting elements of museum education. Interpretation can include the cultural origin of the artifact and the connections to be made between visitors and the object. The ever-present challenge is to motivate people to learn and to keep them interested. When conducting tours, guides can do more than give information to visitors; they can interpret the information through proven teaching techniques and strategies.

BARRIERS TO LEARNING

Visitors are sometimes put off by imposing or unfamiliar museum buildings, especially when they did not frequent them as children. Institutions can ease the transition from the outside world into the exhibits by providing appealing entries, clear directories, and easily understood information. If guided tours are offered at established times, the schedule for them should be prominently displayed at entrances to the museums.

Museum interiors may also seem strange or threatening. Some people think of art museums, particularly, as mysterious places of culture, a holdover attitude developed years earlier when only the upper classes were welcomed. Also, for many people, stresses can build up during the time that they are in the museum. Nelson Graburn (1977) feels that exhibits "demand attention at a pace not experienced elsewhere: it is the burden of the decision-making that falls upon the visitor, because . . . the tempo is . . . controlled by the attendee himself" (p. 23). Decisions have to be made about whether to read labels, move with or against crowds, go to this or that exhibit, and sometimes, the confusion associated with the entire visit makes it unpleasant.

We must consider, too, that effective learning will be impeded when guides prepare themselves poorly for a tour, visitors hold expectations different from guides regarding the purpose of a tour, physiological states like hunger or fatigue intrude, visitor physical disabilities diminish access to tour and exhibit information, and a tour is longer than visitors anticipate it to be. The latter impediment is particularly dismaying when visitors anticipated that a tour which has taken 45 minutes would last only ten minutes.

In all museums, interpreters can be the bridge between visitors and the museum context and can help them become more comfortable in an unfamiliar environment.

EXHIBITS—A PRIMARY SOURCE OF LEARNING

Because of the variety in museums throughout the world, exhibits, among hundreds of possibilities, may be comprised of natural history dioramas, a series of displays showing life cycles, unusual live animals in natural habitats, displays of computer technology, contemporary art, Victorian clothing, or reproductions of a culture with artifacts from an earlier time. Despite this variety, however, exhibits generally are intended to convey an educational intent or theme. They display unusual or rare objects from a specific source or period, or they educate through the exhibit sequence. Consequently, the first sources of information for developing a tour are the design of the exhibit itself and whatever accompanying material its curator provides.

Museum staff members usually prepare the informational material which is on labels or handouts. In doing so, they must assume some level of understanding and knowledge on the part of the audience. Many museums prepare written material specifically for children as well as for adult visitors. Longer, descriptive labels are called "didactic" (instructive) labels, and are often used in museums where large numbers of visitors are expected to go through unguided. Label content—the vocabulary and terminology, layout, type size, and the sequence of information—influences educational effectiveness. (Labeling and signage are being carefully researched today.) In earlier years, few labels were prepared because collections were intended for scholarly study and there were few visitors. Information about objects then was usually stored in card files.

Some museums offer semistructured, self-guided tours when exhibits are conceived as self-sufficient learning centers. The exhibit may include appealing activities such as computer-operated information areas, displays with moving parts, and certain processes which are demonstrated by staff or volunteers. These activities may be excellent learning experiences; their proximity among the exhibits enhances their teaching value.

STIMULATION FOR LEARNING

The museum or historical institution is in a unique position to create superb learning environments for a variety of audiences. The excitement of contact with original objects, animals, historic or natural environments, and so on, stirs the imagination and creates interest in an object or subject. A remarkable number of people refer to museum experiences during childhood as the primary motivation for their chosen careers. Objects acquire powerful attraction when presented in museum settings, whether or not visitors understand the subject or theme of the exhibit. As every teacher knows, it is the child's imagination which seizes upon the word, the object, and the idea. And, of course, it is the imagination that whispers "what if . . . ?" to the inventor, designer, researcher or artisan.

LEARNING ENVIRONMENTS

We cannot completely control the adult or student visitor's surroundings, but we can regulate potential distractions by our tour techniques. Vincent Lanier, an educator in aesthetics, believes that experiences and objects are seen through personal "screens" or "filters" which influence our perception (1982, p. 5). Although Lanier refers specifically to works of art, the same principles may be applied to most museum objects and environments. Each screen "represents a factor that influences how one sees . . . [an object] or what one thinks about as he looks. . ." (p. 5). Settings of objects, as well as the overall museum environment, can help or hinder learning.

It appears that people are easily confused when the environment is strange to them. Research has shown, for example, that when students are put into new environments they can be distracted by the array of stimuli. When they are familiar with an environment or are prepared for a new one, they show gains (over unprepared students) in knowledge presented during structured learning activities. They are more attentive and task-oriented (Falk, Martin and Balling, 1978). Field trips to museums are certainly new environments, with plentiful stimuli; therefore, meaningful learning may not take place without adequate tour preparation. The case for providing an orientation for museum field trips is strong. It is equally strong for providing an orientation for every visitor who walks through the door.

LEARNING STRUCTURES

"The museum is a stage on which a production is presented which allows the visitor the freedom of movement, thought and timing, to interpret the representations in their own familiar terms" (Graburn, 1977, p. 18). Learning structures in museums can be separated into two types which we call, respectively, Formal Learning and Informal Learning. We now consider both types of learning.

INFORMAL LEARNING

Informal Learning: Unguided and random viewing of exhibits.

This kind of learning occurs all the time, consciously and unconsciously, through observation, and experience. It happens as visitors walk around the museum looking at the exhibits, reading labels, or listening to tapes; they participate, for the most part, in self-guided, self-directed activities.

Informal learning is passive and less interactive than formal learning, for it consists mainly of responding or reacting to the environment. (Reading labels or listening to tapes could be called a kind of formal learning because visitors do assimilate prepared information. However, visitors themselves decide whether to interrupt or digress from the learning process.) Museums can present informal learning in many ways: labels, tours on tape, signs, and so forth. Visitors may not think that they are "learning" because they are not being instructed in a traditional sense. At one extreme, informal learning is visitors wandering through exhibits randomly, seldom stopping to consider in detail any source of information.

An informal learning environment is one in which visitors in a museum or historic site are completely on their own. They determine for themselves where to go, what exhibit to look at, and how long to linger. Most visitors expect to learn at museums, and usually read some explanations, didactic labels, and posters as they move through the exhibits. Exhibit labeling is "informal," even though it is designed to lead visitors from one exhibit idea to another. Of course, it is equally possible to spend an afternoon in the museum simply because it is such a pleasant place, where the surroundings are inspiring. People "spending" time may not attempt to take in much information.

Some institutions encourage visitors to interpret exhibits for themselves and help them gain knowledge on their own. Information cards about each object can be found at the Margaret Woodbury Museum in Rochester, New York. At Williamsburg and Old Sturbridge Village, visitors are observers of authentically reproduced environments, and can watch daily life as it would have occurred several centuries ago (Schlereth, 1984). A fairly recent addition to interpretation is the use of actors who can represent, in conversation and action, the people of the century or time being depicted. The Plimoth Plantation staff uses seventeenth century dialect when they are in costume. At Beechwood, the Newport, Rhode Island, estate of Caroline Astor, members of a theatre company take the roles of servants, debutantes, and other personalities who might have been in Astor's life. Visitors are welcomed as Mrs. Astor's guests, and they interact with the "staff" and other "guests." The butler and maid may even have a "disagreement" in front of the visitors. The script reveals insights into life during that period, and information about it is shared by means other than the written word or lecture.

An overview of tours and techniques centered on informal learning:

1. object gallery: a gallery or room with objects or artifacts placed

around it in a manner designed to enhance the object.

2. orientation gallery: an introductory area which presents information about the exhibit immediately adjacent to it.
3. labels: identification or detailed information about each object. Some labels have several sections, with text increasing in detail.
4. audio-tours: tapes that follow through an exhibit sequentially. Some tapes are activated by a small transmitter at the object, which allows visitors to choose objects which are of interest to them.
5. signs: these guide visitors from one exhibit to the next, or identify exhibits and areas.
6. interactive exhibits: found most often in science and children's museums. At many interactive exhibits visitors can operate mechanical or electrical devices which initiate special lighting effects, supply answers, or provide choices among several performance options.
7. field trips: these are usually associated more with formal than informal learning, but under some circumstances they can be quite informal. For example, many schools and adult groups visit museums on their own. They do not have guided tours, nor do they have any preparation for their visit. Therefore, they must depend on labels, signs, and whatever other information that is supplied.

FORMAL LEARNING

Formal Learning: involves planned objectives; exhibit viewing is usually structured by tour guides. True formal learning takes place when visitors either listen to or work with interpreters or participate in structured or semistructured activities designed for their education. In other words, formal learning occurs when visitors are guided through a planned activity, which is intended to add to their understanding or sharpen their perceptions. Participants do not really have the option of ending the instructional process unless they walk away. Guided tours, workshops, lectures, school projects, discussions, and slide presentations fall in this category.

The formal learning environment is one in which the visitor or group of visitors participates in planned learning. All planned tours with docents or tour guides may be considered "formal learning." Formal learning tour techniques include: Lecture (the most structured and rigid of the techniques), and those we identify as Lecture-Discussion, Inquiry-Discussion, Guided Discovery, and Guided Involvement (See Chapter Five).

We might think of some children's museums as "semistructured," since signs or attractive, colorful exhibits "guide" the children. But each unit the children are exposed to is, in reality, structured. Students may feel they have choices; however, they are prompted by subtle cues provided in the area by the museum. When attractive graphics are used to "tell" children what to do, their impact can be very strong, and sometimes, the delivery or presentation takes on a greater significance than the message.

An overview of tours centered on formal learning:

1. Lectures: a one-directional format in which information is provided by a leader. It allows limited group participation.
2. Guided tours: these are led by a trained interpreter or staff member, following a planned procedure (See Chapter Five).
3. Workshops: these are group sessions in which members participate through active involvement. Workshops can be used for skill learning or for interacting with other group members. Audiences may be mixed by age, interests, and so forth.
4. School projects: these are for students who are directed by guides and teachers to accomplish learning objectives. Students may function individually, in teams, or as a large group. Guides and teachers usually confer in planning.
5. Audio-visual presentations: used for introducing exhibits, or programs about a subject. They are usually moderated by an interpreter or staff member, who will lead a discussion.

We may recall that learning occurs in all situations, including times during which we play and have fun. Enjoyable experiences during a tour will promote learning. Following a good formal, or structured tour, heightened curiosity may lead to further exploration of exhibits.

THE LEARNING FOCUS

The focus for learning in museums is the objects, whether art, artifacts, animals, trees, geysers, cars, or textiles. When introducing objects to visitors, guides may use two approaches, separately or together. The **Object-Directed** method is solely concerned with the object, in and of itself. Any peripheral information is subjugated to the task of viewing and contemplating the object. The **Object-Associated** method, in contrast, relates the object to a cultural, historical, or personal reference, creating and enlarging the context of the object.

OBJECT-DIRECTED

The strategy of looking at an object purely for color, line, form, or other aesthetic concerns we call Object-Directed. Although this strategy is used most often in art museums and can be thought of as an aesthetic approach, it can be applied to any object we are examining. For example, the colorations of birds, the line and pattern in various cacti, or the different shades of green in conifer and deciduous forests are all legitimate perceptions for object analysis.

Guides can help develop visual sensitivity and observation skills in children by helping them to see and analyze an object (Madeja, 1977). Edmund Burke Feldman classifies aspects of this process as description, formal analysis, interpretation, and evaluation (Feldman, 1967, p. 295). In some tour techniques, visitors can be personally engaged in seeing, touching, and evaluating (a replica or an authentic piece), thus extending their perceptual experiences. When viewing an object for its own sake, visitors must learn how to "see" the artifact, which involves perception of form, color, line, texture, pattern, and other aesthetic elements. However, as visitors learn more about the objects, they may be better able to perceive and appreciate aesthetic qualities.

The touring method called "object-oriented," as practiced throughout American museums today, is a concept which is more global than our notion of "Object-Directed." However, all touring is object-oriented, since objects **are** the contents of museums.

OBJECT-ASSOCIATED

It is difficult for objects to become significant by themselves, as the discussion in Chapter Three on concept formation reveals. Effective interpretation relates an exhibit or object to its cultural setting or to relevant aspects of visitors' personal experiences. Individuality and uniqueness in exhibits and objects are important, but wider implications should also be drawn from them. John Fines, a British historian and noted museum educator focuses on single objects. However, he uses them to "explore humanity" and go beyond the object to its wider meaning (Fines, 1982). The environments of Boston's Faneuil Hall Marketplace and Baltimore's redevelopment area, designed by Ben Thompson of the Harvard Graduate School of Design, were developed with this philosophy in mind. These areas "work" because people of all ages use them for many purposes and, therefore, are comfortable in those settings. They relate their experiences in the Boston or Baltimore areas to pleasurable experiences, real or fictional, and thus, to a wider context. The areas in Boston and Baltimore are fascinating, aesthetic environments, as well as historic.

Museum objects cannot be appreciated in a vacuum. Visitors need to be supplied with associations and references. When viewing objects in cultural settings, Thomas Schlereth, in his book **Material Culture Studies in America,** suggests nine conceptual models to help visitors gain knowledge (Schlereth, 1984). Each model indicates a different way of interpreting objects, suggests unique problems, and brings out novel properties of the object. The nine models are noted below.

1. art history
2. symbolist
3. cultural history
4. environmentalist
5. functionalist

6. structuralist
7. behavioristic
8. national character
9. social history

If guides were to interpret, for example, a wooden duck decoy using these models, visitors would obtain a great many insights about the object. For example, the decoy could be seen as an art form, as symbolic of American folk art, as a useful item for hunting, as a negative influence on the shorebird population, as a lure to attract other birds, as a means to get food or feathers, and so on. Thus, we can see that the same object can mean entirely different things to the beholder, depending upon the interpretation made of it.

It is thus preferable to increase the number of ways visitors look at given objects. It does visitors little good to pass by many different artifacts superficially. In tour planning, guides might list questions that fit Schlereth's categories in order to generate further ideas for discussion. This procedure strengthens the learning experience for visitors as they are given opportunities to think about objects in different ways.

LEARNING METHODS FOR TOURS

When visitors are actively involved while touring, they will be able to understand how objects are related, how the objects relate to themselves personally, and how they fit into different contexts. Examples of methods that involve visitors during tours include Comparison and Contrast, Imagination, and by Thematic Emphasis. Each of these methods is described below. Each represents an especially useful strategy for all of the tour techniques discussed in Chapter Six.

COMPARISON AND CONTRAST

Comparing and contrasting are important methods in tours, for when viewing two objects that are similar in some way, their different qualities can be clarified. This method may be used with as many objects or exhibits as time will allow. The examples selected should be representative of the tour objectives. By comparing and contrasting, visitors will learn to refine perceptual skills that will help them analyze the different elements of the objects. Interpreters may choose objects that are similar in several ways, but they should select some objects that are clearly unrepresentative as a contrast to those that have similarities. Contrasts are as important for clarity of understanding as are similarities. Visitors should then be encouraged to seek for themselves examples that have similar or different qualities. Preschool age children need to have explicit examples;

the "comparison" method helps them isolate qualities and learn to classify objects.

IMAGINATION

Children use their imaginations effectively to think about things which are not present and to fantasize about that which cannot really happen. They are not bound by adult conventions and can propel discussion into unanticipated areas. For example, a group looking at telegraphs, telephones, or modems can imagine fantastic ways for people to communicate. Imagining helps children be venturesome in their thinking. It lets them come up with new (and old) connections without adult assistance. They must feel free to guess, probe, take risks, and challenge. Role-playing and creative dramatics can also be used, if imagining is to comprise a large part of the tour. Games of imagination can combine fun with learning.

THEMATIC EMPHASIS

Tours can be developed around a single or common theme. Thematic tours, in many instances, can be more effective than those with narrow learning objectives (see Schlereth's conceptual models). A broad learning objective, for a zoo or natural history museum, could be the "houses" of animals. A learning goal could be to compare and contrast nests, lairs, burrows, or man-made items which illustrate the objective. The supporting objects or exhibits can be drawn from varied collections. In this manner, children are able to contemplate possibilities and draw from their experiences. They also begin to understand the more abstract ideas of protection, warmth, raising of families, and so on. Consider a few other themes that can be made either simple or complex:

1. Science museums: a physiological theme; or the impact of machines on town, city, or country.
2. Art museums: a particular historical period or school of painting; decorative objects; effect of war, social class on the history of sculpture.
3. Natural history museums: interrelationship of living creatures in specific environments (tropical, temperate, coastal, etc.); effect of heat, sun on plants.
4. History museums or restored buildings: a particular period; influence of trade or climate on town, region, or an individual family.

Themes are able to cut across time periods and remove ideas from their usual contexts. Any subject can benefit from a broad objective or theme.

Museum learning is different from that of the classroom because it teaches visitors from objects in exhibits and from other material. Objects and the way they are exhibited are unique sources of stimulation and learning. Museum environments can be intimidating; guides can prepare visitors during the warm-up for the tour to come. Museums also can have welcoming entries with clear directions. During the tour, guides should consider carefully how the tour material is being presented. Informal learning is the structure that includes tours that are random, individual, and unguided. Most tours in museums are formal in structure and are preplanned. Within tours, if Object-Directed information is presented, it should accompany an Object-Associated focus. The latter is particularly important, as details about the objects are unlikely to be interesting and important to visitors unless they are culturally relevant and relate to the visitors' lives.

REFERENCES

Falk, J. M., Martin, W. W., & Balling, J. D. (1978). The novel field trip phenomenon: adjustment to novel settings interferes with task learning. **Journal of Research in Science Teaching, 15,** 127-34. (Cited in Roundtable Reports, 1982, 7(4), 18.)

Feldman, E. B. (1967). **Art as Image and Idea.** Englewood Cliffs, N.J.: Prentice-Hall.

Fines, J. (1982). Imagination in teaching—reflections on my fortnight's work. **Roundtable Reports: The Journal of Museum Education. 7**(2). Washington, DC: Museum Education Roundtable, 3-10.

Graburn, N. H. H. (1977). The museum and the visitor experience. In L. Draper (Ed.) **The Visitor and The Museum,** 5-26. Washington, DC: American Association of Museums.

Lanier, V. (1983). The arts we see: where it's coming from. **In Perspective: The Journal of the Arizona Art Education Association, 1**(4), 4-8. (From **The Visual Arts We See: A Simplified Introduction to the Visual Arts,** 1982. New York: Teachers College Press, Columbia University. 69-90.)

Madeja, S. S. (1977). The child and aesthetic development. In **Proceedings from The Arts and Handicapped People: Defining the National Direction Conference,** (p. 31-36). Washington, DC: The National Committee, Arts for the Handicapped.

Schlereth, T. (1984). Object knowledge: every museum visitor an interpreter. **Roundtable Reports: The Journal of Museum Education. 9**(1), 5-9. Washington, DC: Museum Education Roundtable.

PART TWO–THE INTERPRETIVE PROCESS

CHAPTER FIVE
Techniques of Interpretation

Getting Organized • Interpretive Techniques • Questioning Strategies • Tour Aids • Supplemental Tour Information • Tour Problems

GETTING ORGANIZED

Visitors to museums differ so greatly in their interests and learning styles that museums offer them a variety of educational options. Some people prefer to read long labels, some like taped tours, others choose written self-guides, and still others prefer tours guided by docents. Among the educational options, the guided tour is best suited for matching exhibit content with the needs and interests of visitors. Guided tours are most successful when both considerations are given careful attention. Therefore, effective tour design requires that the facets of content and the methods of presentation be integrated.

THE NEED FOR PLANNING

The agony visitors feel after a poorly conducted tour tends to remain for a long time. Too often, people move slowly around a gallery filled with small objects, each of which is treated with equal importance by their guide. Facts are rarely connected as the tour progresses from object to object. The guide may assume that the group is there because they already know something, for example, about China, crabs, or the Victorian house. Time drags by, and the guide cannot end the tour because there is nothing to summarize. An announcement that time is up and a request for questions is the typical ending of such a tour.

Interpretation of objects, collections, and historic sites deserves more. The significance of objects can be clarified by including details, first, about an individual object (who made it, how it was made, and a review of its aesthetic elements), and, second, about the cultural context in which the object was developed (why it was made, how it was used, what value and meaning it had). Obviously, facts about both objects and their contexts should be taken into account when selecting items or sites for educational purposes. The best tours are those that are preplanned with selection of objectives, content, and method of presentation based on the characteristics of the visitors to be toured. When information about tour groups is insufficient, or their reasons for coming to the museum are unknown, guides might contact teachers or group leaders for guidance. (This practice may prevent subsequent misunderstanding.) Some teachers use field trips for museum "exposure," for example, and only want their students to see an overview of the collections. Such teachers would be disappointed by a tour guide who set tour objectives for an in-depth presentation of a few exhibits.

One strategy for avoiding misunderstandings is to confer with the teacher and, then, send previsit information to the school so that visitors will know something about the subject matter before their arrival. Museum guides also can learn subject requirements from curriculum guides for each school grade level, and in using this information, they can develop specific tours suitable for the different grade levels. The prepared tours might focus on a culture (Egypt), or objects (suits of armor), or a defined area (Expressionist painting). A selection of them may be sent to the schools for teachers to choose from. The teachers may also wish to request a tour tailored particularly to their educational objectives. Visitors who are prepared for a tour, whether students or adults, are more likely to respond positively to the museum experience and to interact at more informed levels.

OUTLINE PREPARATION

A tour should be divided into three parts: objective(s), content or subject matter, and conclusion(s). In filling out the skeleton of the tour outline, tour guides should work from the following definitions:

1. The tour objective(s): what, precisely, the group should know after the tour is over.

2. The content: the subject matter by which the objective is explained and illustrated. (Examples that support attainment of the objective should be selected from available material. This is like using a road map to find the shortest route from A to B.)
3. The conclusion(s): a review of the information presented to the group, and a summary of how it helps in attaining the objectives. (To help a group in knowing whether an objective has been reached, tour guides might plan an activity, discussion, or questioning period near the end of the tour.)

OBJECTIVES

Objectives are statements that describe what interpreters want visitors to understand and learn. They constitute the framework of the tour. To ensure manageability, only one or two related objectives should be presented in any given tour. Selection of the objectives must be chosen with a specific audience in mind. They should be formulated early in the tour plan, and, as shown below, they should be phrased in "active" verbs, which make them easier for guides to think through and carry out.

1. Visitors will recognize visual symbols used in images of the Buddha.
2. Visitors will identify how architecture is used in painting.
3. Students will see four aspects of a 19th century agricultural village and understand their interdependence.
4. Students will be able to describe leaves of the oak, sugar maple, and tamarack trees.
5. Visitors will be able to identify the square knot, half-hitch knot, and slip-knot.
6. Visitors will be able to identify paintings by Van Gogh.

The advantages of specific wording are several: objectives are clarified, learning goals may be selected more easily, and all content is directed toward achieving them.

Objectives may be abstract and broad (understand architecture in painting) or concrete and specific (identify knots, describe leaves, identify Van Gogh's work).

An abstract objective is focused on ideas that go beyond specifics. History and art museums frequently use abstract objectives for adolescent and adult tours. Examples of abstract objectives are "understanding how religious art was used for teaching" or "how nationalism inspires artistic endeavors." Abstract objectives are sometimes more difficult than those relatively concrete to communicate and understand.

A concrete objective is centered on learning something about an actual "practice" or a particular thing. Knowledge of concrete things usually can be learned through the senses, i.e., can be seen, touched, heard, tasted, or smelled. Some examples of concrete tour objectives might be "to identify plants that people can use for food or clothing;" "to observe how cloth is made from fibre to fabric;" "to learn that art objects are created from many different materials or media." (See Chapter Three, "How People Learn," for more information on the distinctions between "concrete" and "abstract.")

LEARNING GOALS

Learning goals support objectives and provide definition to the steps used to accomplish them. Any number of objects may be used to enhance learning goals pertaining to a single objective. Learning about the objects should be organized in logical progression. For example, guides can demonstrate the distinguishing characteristics of the eohippus (through comparison with other animals) before identifying the similarities and differences between the eohippus and the contemporary horse. Another example would be to have visitors view several examples of Van Gogh's painting style, noting similarities, before comparing them with styles of other painters. Therefore, tour guides might develop learning goals in relation to objectives as follows:

1. Objective: The visitor will be able to identify paintings by Van Gogh.
   Learning goals:
   a. Compare two or more paintings by Van Gogh (information about the artist's life and motivation may be given here).
   b. Compare and contrast one painting by Van Gogh with one or more paintings by other artists, noting color, composition, paint thickness, and so forth.
   c. Find paintings by Van Gogh, with similar characteristics.

2. Objective: Students will be able to identify evolutionary changes in the horse.
   Learning goals:
   a. Compare and contrast an eohippus and a horse by diagrams, models, or skeletons.
   b. Emphasize progressive changes from the eohippus to the modern horse through comparing and contrasting successive models.

3. Objective: The visitor will be able to understand and recognize a variety of artistic media.
   Learning goals:
   a. Select three or four examples: weaving, oil painting, sculpture, prints.
   b. Explain significant similarities and differences (process, history, use, etc.)
   c. Handle (physically) and describe examples of different media.
   d. Review and identify examples of each in the collection.

4. Objective: The visitor will identify how architecture is used in painting.
   Learning goals:
   a. Select paintings that include architectural detail.
   b. Explain similarities and differences.
   c. Isolate examples of romantic ideals in architecture.
   d. Discuss neo-classical influence on American public buildings.

When selecting objects to help attain the learning goals and to illustrate an objective of the tour, the best possible examples should be chosen. This does not mean that the objects selected are the most valuable, or the most representative, but that they are the ones that complement the learning goals and support the objective. For example, when children tour a history museum, the topic might be "Listening Long Ago." The children could discuss, with the interpreter, the sounds that children might have heard fifty years ago. Examples of the sounds could be drawn from exhibits that present early farms, delivery wagons, steam trains, automobiles, and radios.

The learning goals used in most of the foregoing examples are appropriate for younger visitors, or those having little or no background in the subject. For older students or adults, the concrete objectives might serve as learning goals and new, more challenging abstract objectives might be created for them.

The guides' task, then, is to expand upon the learning goals as a way of meeting the selected objectives. A tour may be likened to a symphony, whereby the sonata form, an element in the first movement, appears again in each part of the symphony. The sonata form, for example, "has three sections (1) exposition, or statement of the theme; (2) development, or restatement and presentation of thematic materials from a variety of points of view; and (3) recapitulation, a restatement and summary of previously presented materials" (Lessinger and Gillis, 1976, p. 89).

In respect to the sonata metaphor, the objectives of the tour are like the "theme" of a sonata and the learning goals and content represent development of the theme from a variety of points of view.

TOUR BACKGROUND MATERIALS

Interpreters need to have sound, personal knowledge of each exhibit or object to be used during touring. Much information can be gathered from studying the objects. Unfamiliar objects encountered on a tour sometimes can be identified by making educated guesses, but the only way to be certain is to have information before the tour about all objects likely to be included in it. Considerable time should be spent in the museum beforehand, looking at familiar objects carefully, and then, again with "new eyes." Advance study may help guides think of new tour approaches and questions that will inspire discussion. Also, as many exhibit areas change from time to time, guides at all times need to maintain a working knowledge of the exhibit areas. Reference lists of objectives, tour questions, and pertinent information about exhibits are invaluable for advance tour planning. Data could be divided by gallery, topic, types of objects, culture, chronology, or any other meaningful category. The preparation of informative background notes about exhibits can help guides create new ways to present the collections, and avoid the kind of sterile tours that result from memorization of facts.

New questions and ideas can be developed from notes. A notebook developed around the following reference points might include:

1. to emphasize the objects (Object-Directed Information)—data about important features, including specific details.
   a. the aesthetic properties in the materials, design, form, texture, color, line, or craftsmanship. (Applicable to all man-made and natural objects.)
   b. how objects are used to fulfill learning goals and an objective.

2. to emphasize the context (Object-Associated information)—data about cultural, historical, technical aspects of objects.
   a. important facts about the background of the objects.
   b. connections between objects and individual activities and/or society in general.
   c. ways objects are similar to or different from other objects in the collection. Use nearby objects for comparisons and contrasts.

3. to use with tour objectives—include information about specific objects pertinent to objectives.
   a. review and contrast objects to determine whether they support the learning goals and objectives.
   b. compare given features across a wide variety of examples.

INTERPRETIVE TECHNIQUES

After establishing the objectives, the learning goals, and the artifacts or exhibits to be used, guides need to consider the interpretive technique which will work most successfully.

The best tour method for real learning and enjoyment is an interactive one. The visitors' background, existing knowledge, ideas, and questions form the bases for what and how they learn. Visitors, in effect, should do their own thinking and analyses while interpreters "guide" discussion.

Three basic techniques for guiding visitors in museums may be adapted to suit almost any group. These are "interpretive techniques." They structure the way in which tour content is presented to visitors. Guides may choose among them for the one most appropriate to the characteristics of the visitor group. Under certain circumstances, interpreters also may move from one strategy to another during a tour.

The three interpretive techniques to be described in detail in this section are:

Lecture-Discussion
Inquiry-Discussion
Guided Discovery

The following discussion provides detailed suggestions for developing each of these interpretive techniques. Group profiles in Chapter Six will help determine which technique is most likely to be successful for a particular group. Tour guides should feel free, however, to borrow from other strategies whenever a tour requires it.

For each of the interpretive techniques guides should

1. have accurate information about objects used in the tour; they should know the correct pronunciation for all names and terms; they should be aware of the cultural background of the objects and know all pertinent technical information about them.
2. be able to provide information at several learning levels, considering visitors' age, knowledge, preparation, and so forth.
3. know more about the objects than can be presented in one tour. Interpreters, thereby, will have flexibility in choosing which aspects of information to use and a store of knowledge for answering questions from the group.
4. be able to group and regroup objects together to serve a variety of objectives. For example, a Renaissance painting may serve as an example of portraits, religious symbolism, technical use of oil paints, Renaissance humanism, artistic freedom, artistic patronage, motherhood, and so forth. The painting might be discussed in one or all of these categories to attain different objectives.

THE LECTURE-DISCUSSION TECHNIQUE

The Lecture-Discussion tour, in contrast with those of Inquiry-Discussion and Guided Discovery, presents information within an instructional format that provides limited opportunity for visitor-guide interaction. The technique is useful in surveys of the museum's collections for groups with limited time. Guides do most of the talking. Questions are welcomed, however, and visitors are encouraged to participate in discussions. This technique is particularly suitable for high school and adult groups because people in these age groups, relative to younger age groups, will have greater background knowledge and responsiveness to in-depth information. It is unsuited for younger age groups because the

Lecture-Discussion format cannot hold the attention of young people across the average length of a tour. However, older groups may also respond poorly to questions—unless they have a special interest in the topic, know one another well, or, if they are students, have been encouraged by their teachers to respond freely to questioning. Tour groups will be unpredictable in their responsiveness to discussion, so interpreters should be prepared to present "lecture" material throughout the entire tour.

With the Lecture-Discussion technique, visitors should have some time for independent touring at the conclusion of the tour. In this way, information learned during the tour may be applied to the exhibits individually.

The success of the Lecture-Discussion technique depends upon the guides' knowledge of the subject, ability to organize ideas into a commentary that has continuity, and public speaking and communication skills. But Lecture-Discussion also includes some interaction with the audience. Minimal interaction might involve requesting information about the group during the introduction period, and then, adopting lecture techniques. A more preferable level of interaction involves encouraging questions and discussion during the tour. Such a strategy is far more effective for teaching and changing attitudes than a monologue.

In general, guides who use the Lecture-Discussion technique should look not linger over objects; visitors will be more alert and observant if the lecture is pertinent and moves along steadily. Proceeding to another location, changing the pattern of information, telling an anecdote, becoming more energetic in body language—any such changes of pace may revive a lagging lecture. Personal communication skills are important in establishing rapport with groups and projecting enthusiasm during tours. In the lecture situation, guides must encourage a sense of unity within the group. An easy, informal attitude is preferable to a formal or aloof style of presentation.

OUTLINE FOR THE LECTURE-DISCUSSION TECHNIQUE

The Warm-up. The warm-up is a short period during which visitors prepare for the tour by adjusting to the group, the situation, and the guide's tour style. The warm-up for the Lecture-Discussion technique consists of a personal introduction, a welcome to the museum, and questions to the group regarding their knowledge about the subject and their specific interests. Guides might discuss briefly both the tour objectives (what the tour will accomplish), and the tour learning goals (how the objectives will be achieved). This will prepare the audience for following the lecture more easily. Guides should then describe how the tour will proceed and introduce the tour content, as it pertains to the museum exhibits.

The Objectives. As we have learned, objectives and learning goals are common to each tour technique. They provide the structure to which all the information and methods must adhere. Objectives and learning goals should be preplanned, so that the lecture has coherence and logical progression. The objectives may be introduced by questions which relate to the visitors' own experiences and, thus, stimulate their interest. Guides can then present the objectives in response to visitors' answers. For example, one way to introduce adult visitors to a collection of porcelain or silver objects might be as follows:

Q: Can you think of dishes we use for different occasions, such as picnics or camping?

A: Paper plates, aluminum (unbreakable dishes), "company" dishes.

or

Q: Why don't you use your grandmother's dishes more frequently on such occasions?

A: It is too much trouble to handle them carefully and wash them by hand.

Guides might center their responses to either introductory question around the following issues: the desire of people to find convenient, time-saving ways of doing things, the fact that most people do not have household help, and the many responsibilities that women have outside the home. Insight for all of these perspectives may be discussed in terms of another period or culture. Why, for example, were decorative, functional objects like dishes cared for so well that they still exist today for us to enjoy and study?

The implications of the above introductory questions may seem obvious. But such simple questions as "why don't we take good dishes on picnics" will not be viewed as moronic by adults or silly by younger age groups, providing tour guides help them imagine the underlying cultural significance of answers to such questions.

The Questions. Questions are used with the Lecture-Discussion technique to add interest and to change the pace of a tour. They are not as vital to tour development and success as they are in the Inquiry-Discussion technique. Asking questions offers variation and makes visitors think about the subject at hand. Open-ended questions—those with many possible answers—promote new dimensions of thinking. Questions should be used to direct visitors' attention to specific attributes of objects during the lecture. Ending the tour with an open-ended question may encourage visitors to remember and think about what was discussed. Questions probably will generate answers in visitors' minds, even though they may never answer them verbally.

Conclusion. The Lecture-Discussion technique concludes with a summary of the points covered, a restatement of the objective(s), and a request for questions. The group may be invited now to move through the exhibition individually, so that they can apply the information they have heard both to the exhibits they just toured and to new exhibits. If possible, guides should remain in the area so as to be available for further discussion.

THE INQUIRY-DISCUSSION TECHNIQUE

The Inquiry-Discussion technique is a dialogue tour which consists of questions, answers, and discussion between guides and visitors. Visitors explore ideas and relationships under a guide's direction while observing exhibits and objects. Guides give background information and facts at appropriate intervals during the discussion. Questions are used as a means to direct discussion toward the attainment of tour objectives. The Inquiry-Discussion technique is the one most satisfactory for groups in general, for it invites interaction at all levels of learning. It is especially successful with student groups and is a natural format for children, where the technique enables guides to draw upon children's natural curiosity and zest for new ideas and experiences.

The Inquiry-Discussion technique requires that guides be discussion leaders, not lecturers. As tour facilitators, they need to be open and responsive. Inquiry-Discussion is the technique most likely to change visitors' attitudes (affective learning) because it builds upon their own interests, perceptions, responses, and questions. The structure for attaining insights and new knowledge is shifted from the guide's lecture to group discussion. Visitors also have the opportunity to hear and learn about the ideas of others in their group. Interpreters must direct their questions towards specific objectives, and they must control the direction in which discussion may go.

Questions and the interaction they generate give guides/interpreters opportunity to volunteer information. They must present it concisely, enthusiastically, and at a level the group can understand. The discussion and interjected information should be directed toward moving the group along to new levels of thought. Guides should have sufficient historical and technical knowledge to provide "settings" for the objects. Specific facts, such as accurate historical references, which are used frequently in the Lecture-Discussion technique, may be less important than the general background of a culture, period, or scientific concept. General notions about influences upon change, technological advances, or ways in which objects were used or made, can broaden understanding more than a series of specific, but perhaps, unrelated facts. Of course, whenever exhibitions, historical sites, or scientific discoveries can be identified with important people, references to the specific facts of their contributions can enliven discussion.

During the Inquiry-Discussion tour, the real possibility exists that the direction of a tour will become altered by visitors' questions. However, the preplanned objectives should not be abandoned. The order of the tour should be adjusted to ensure that they are attained.

OUTLINE FOR INQUIRY-DISCUSSION TECHNIQUE

The Warm-up. Guides can establish rapport with visitors while identifying each group's needs, interests, and general knowledge about the subject. The warm-up informs a group about what to expect from the tour, and in this instance, sets the tone for informal discussion. Guides should indicate to visitors that they will be sharing tour experiences with them, serving as "directors" for touring and discussions, and supplying information to them whenever it is needed. It is especially important that visitors understand that all of their questions and answers are appropriate and that they will be encouraged to ask them during the tour.

First, guides should introduce themselves, giving the names by which they expect to be addressed. Some brief, personal information helps establish an informal mood. Guides might mention how much they enjoy learning about history (or different cultures, art, geology, animals, the environment, etc.), or how much tours give them opportunity to share exciting aspects of the museum with others.

Second, the warm-up offers opportunity for general questions by both guides and group members. Guides' questions should involve the visitors and stress personal interest in them. Warm-up questions for student groups, for example, might include:

1. Have you studied this subject? If so, what was the most exciting thing you learned?
2. What would you like to know? Why?
3. Tell me something important you know about this subject.
4. Have you visited this museum before? If so, what did you like best? Why?
5. Have you heard that we have something special here? What would you like to see most?

More personally oriented warm-up questions for adults and children might focus on their experiences and interests.

1. How many of you have tried to grow plants (paint a picture, weave, build a chair, carve a piece of wood, care for an animal, start a collection, keep a journal, write a story, etc.)? Such a question relates the tour topic to the visitors' personal experiences.
2. Is there anything you have seen on a previous visit that you want to see again?
3. What are your hobbies? (It is always helpful when these relate to tour objectives.)

Third, the warm-up should also include directions to visitors about what to expect during the tour. When groups are large, guides should make clear that each person will be given time to look at the exhibits under discussion before the group moves on to the next one. Visitors will thereby listen more carefully to the discussion and be less inclined to scurry about, trying in the middle of something to see everything.

The Objectives. Questions can be used to present the tour objectives, as in the Lecture-Discussion technique, and to provoke interest. For example: Have any of you ever made a clay pot? Can you imagine how the wet, soft clay would feel in your hands? Did you know that fine china is made from special kinds of clay? Answers to these questions can be used to begin a short discussion about different, but familiar objects made of clay. Tour subjects may be as diverse as pre-Columbian figure sculpture, Native American pottery, Renaissance terracotta figurines, Chinese porcelains, and Egyptian tomb figures and artifacts. The objectives associated with questions about clay might be to discover the different ways clay has been used and decorated and to discuss the culture in which the clay objects were made. Visitors will learn that through history and in the present, clay has been and is being used to create functional, decorative, art objects.

Questions During the Tour. During the Inquiry-Discussion technique, guides should use questions to direct attention to the important aspects of each object which help support attainment of the objective. The Inquiry-Discussion tour is based on questions which build further dialogue. Information is given by guides to advance the discussion. Questions of two types are used throughout this tour technique to involve visitors. The kinds of answers they yield help guides become aware of the levels at which the group is understanding the objectives. The two types of questions are "Object-Directed" (convergent) and "Object-Associated" (divergent). They can be used interchangeably in a single tour. Object-Directed questions focus discussion on the object and elicit information about detail. Object-Associated questions focus discussion on object usefulness, ramifications for society, and aesthetic values for both original makers and visitors. These are the questions that bring forth information about cultural context. (See Chapter Four, "Museums and Learning" for further discussion about "Object-Directed" and "Object-Associated" learning.) Involving visitors through questions about both details and contexts helps ensure that all tour members are acquiring a uniform understanding of the tour content. Specific questioning techniques are discussed later in this chapter.

Conclusion. Time should be allowed at the end of the tour for a summary of the tour and its objectives. Visitors may be asked to find other exhibits that pertain to the objectives and to indicate why they are good examples. The group can be dispersed for a "brief looking time" in the gallery areas and brought together again for a final discussion. Another way to summarize the Inquiry-Discussion tour is to ask questions of the group which requests their ideas and conclusions. Visitors might be asked what they enjoyed, what they learned most about, and what they would like to see again on their next visit. The visitors' answers will help guides determine whether the tour objectives were attained.

LECTURE-DISCUSSION TECHNIQUE VERSUS INQUIRY-DISCUSSION TECHNIQUE

Talking "with" visitors is more helpful as an educational strategy than talking "at" visitors. When adults must listen to lectures that they do not understand, they will simply stop listening and pay attention to distractions. Some may stray away from the guide. Lecture tours are often too long; adults seldom attend well to speakers after twenty minutes unless the subject interests them—forty minutes is really the limit. The pure lecture format (in the traditional sense) is the least effective way to present information to museum visitors. Unfortunately, it is also the format used by a great many museum interpreters. Guides often believe that the best use of their time is to provide visitor groups with as much information as possible. Sometimes they choose the lecture format because they are too timid to interact with visitors.

Whenever instruction is provided by lecture, the audience is required to function passively. The lecture format has its place, but there are more effective ways to present an interpretive lecture to a standing audience in museum. To include as much discussion as possible is to provide a basic improvement. The Inquiry-Discussion technique however, will degenerate into a "lecture" if the guide does all of the talking while the audience only listens; a true "discussion" must include both guide and audience participation. Cognitive learning is facilitated through instructional lectures, but affective learning, a change in attitude, is more likely to take place during group discussions (Whitman, 1983, p. 4). Museum interpreters, of course, often encourage cognitive and affective learning simultaneously. Both knowledge and attitudes toward cultural beliefs and behaviors, as noted below, may be changed through museum education.

> *The potential of group discussion to teach new interests, attitudes, and values can be explained by the classic work of Zander (1962) regarding the major principle of overcoming resistance, namely, that people need to develop their own understanding of the need for change with an awareness of how they feel about it and what can be done about those feelings. According to Zander, conditions which help people develop this understanding and awareness include two-way communication, letting people air their feelings, and involving people in gathering relevant facts. These are all activities which can be accomplished in a group discussion (Whitman, 1983, p. 4).*

THE GUIDED DISCOVERY TECHNIQUE

The Guided Discovery technique offers visitors a structured activity in which they determine their own touring directions and connections with the exhibits. Learning by Discovery varies from other tour techniques in that the learning connections often are unanticipated, because only the tour skeleton is supplied by guides. Visitors impose their own pathways within it. Learning can conceivably take place at another time entirely because the concepts gained in the museum setting can trigger learning in another place. Visitors may use all domains of learning at once with this tour technique. Motor, affective, and cognitive learning may occur. What transpires will be affected by the elements of museum exhibits that are prechosen for emphasis by guides.

Tour guides are responsible for establishing a general hypothesis, or subject area "problem," at the beginning of the tour. From this starting point, visitors follow whatever is of particular interest to them. Therefore, people in a tour may begin at the same point and branch out individually into different subject areas. They become actively involved in the tour. For example, the exploration of the daily life of the original occupants of an historic site might encourage people to pursue interests as diverse as furniture (decorative arts), farm equipment (early agriculture), holiday customs (history), the herb garden (cooking and botany), the telegraph office (early communication objects), art (portraiture), the schoolroom (early education), etc.

During a Guided Discovery tour, guides stay in control of the tour, supplying information, stimulating new directions for thought, and monitoring the group's progress. Visitors should not be hunting about for clues. The tour can be a learning experience for guides, too, as they will learn new ideas about the exhibits from the visitors. The visitors, in turn, will be stimulated by the "new" experience of "thinking" in museums. They will be inspired to learn about what interests them rather than to learn facts. They will find their own answers and connections, with the help of the guide. Visitors who participate in this touring method are more likely than those involved in other techniques to become interested and curious when looking at museum exhibits. They are more likely, too, to advance from absorbing specific information to drawing general ideas, that is, engaging in inductive learning. Even though Guided Discovery tours are somewhat structured, they are flexible enough to allow visitors to think and "discover" according to their own frames of reference. Therefore, guides can expect that many relationships among personal views and object characteristics will have to be explored and rejected before conclusions are affirmed.

Another positive attribute of Guided Discovery is that the discovery experience is nonthreatening. It differs from experiences that occur in school and daily life, where individuals anticipate that right answers are expected of them and that others may make judgements about them from the quality of their "answers." Incorrect responses are part of the discovery process, but, in contrast to school and daily life situations, they are not considered "wrong."

The discovery process may not be totally successful for very young children as they do not know how to "solve" problems. However, it is useful for anyone old enough to compare and contrast objects and concepts.

Museums have unique opportunities for replacing didactic methods of teaching, which are used very frequently in school classrooms and for adult museum tours. Using the Guided Discovery technique, for example, visitors can learn to investigate, to use evidence, to evaluate, to form concepts, to see relationships, and to be aware of opposing viewpoints. Students will be challenged by this technique to arrive at new learning experiences that go far beyond merely gathering facts. Guided Discovery can be used with any age group, although it is particularly suitable for students older than age seven and adult groups having special interests. However, Guided Discovery, more than Lecture-Discussion and Inquiry-Discussion, requires imagination, perseverance, and considerable preparation on the part of interpreters and museum educators.

Ideally, Guided Discovery in museums should occur in teams or in small groups of people, and it should be carefully monitored. Individual exploration provides little feedback to visitors, and part of the reward of discovery is reinforcement by group members or via joint conclusion-drawing. The actual "discovery" part of the tour may take as much time as guides wish to devote to it. With adults, it may be preferable to spend some of the time in general discussion. Guides can then help visitors understand the broader concepts that underlie aspects of exhibits.

To be a successful technique, visitors following Guided Discovery should believe that the task given them is solvable, the information at hand is understandable, the challenge of discovery will actively involve them, and the information they will acquire is applicable to the rest of the exhibit. The procedure to be followed in setting up a Guided Discovery tour is similar to that for other tours, except now, information is **available** rather than **provided.** The optimum result of a tour of this type is "positive transfer," where visitors have "the ability to go beyond the data or to go beyond the specifics" (Wittrock, 1966, p. 75). Guides should not feel, therefore, that given objectives must be reached precisely during a tour—unless, of course, a group leader or teacher requests that a specific one be attained.

GUIDED DISCOVERY AND SCHOOL TOURS

Museums are, for the most part, concerned with the processes of learning and the formation of concepts rather than how much is learned. Amount of learning can be difficult to assess in museums; teachers, on the other hand, may expect museums tours for their classrooms to produce learned outcomes. Therefore, museums and schools, in general, may have different expectations of what the tour experience should accomplish. Teachers may be most interested in measurable progress in learning; museums do encourage learning specific knowledge, but they may place greater emphasis on the discovery of general principles about an exhibit or theme.

However, the different goals of museums and schools can be reconciled. Guides can plan a measurable outcome for part of the tour, in response to the school's needs, and include guided discovery activities for other aspects of it. By choosing a theme for the tour, grouping similar and dissimilar exhibits together, and selecting appropriate examples, the tour guide may combine both goals. Guides should try to ensure that the tour information is meaningful to the students and that it is applicable or transferable to problem-solving activities. The ideal way to meet both school and museum objectives is (1) for teachers to suggest objectives that support their curriculum needs, and (2) for guides to use these objectives in creating Guided Discovery tours. Guides should make every effort to meet measurable objectives so that teachers will feel that field trips are worthwhile. When teachers' objectives are no more specific than general cultural exposure, guides should be sufficiently informed about exhibits, grade level curricula in schools, and age characteristics of young people to select reasonably appropriate objectives. With school tours, the final problem-solving explorations could be accomplished in the classroom, after the data "collection" has taken place. Tours, however, should emphasize more than reinforcement of school subjects. Learning will be more efficient when tours are prepared so that the content leads into general principles or concepts of history, of art, or of natural history.

Variations of the "discovery" method of touring have been employed in Great Britain for a number of years. Children investigate on their own and pursue their own interests. An imposed structure assists them in their pursuits, as they investigate objects, use facts and evidence that they bring to the tour, perceive relationships, and evaluate conclusions. The children are used to having choices and working independently. Curiosity plays a part in their activities, and it is used to advantage in the museum setting. Many of the British students have assignments; for example, to take pictures, draw, take notes, or make comments into a tape recorder. Children learn to "see." Information is compiled and taken back to the classroom where the students use it for further investigation. Their teachers are in control of their visits. Before the field trip, teachers supply their classes with materials and documents about the exhibits (School Council, 1972).

In some British schools, work cards are used as follow-up materials. They are in the classroom before and after a museum visit so that children can select their own subjects for study. Answers to the problems thus come from first hand observation. "Real" objects also are used frequently in the classroom, and students acquire an appreciation for authenticity. Some examples of "discovery learning" work cards are:

1. Draw water birds at the London Zoo. Go to the British Museum and look at the way Greek artists drew birds on their pots.
2. Play silhouettes with your classmates. Cut out silhouettes of any-

thing of interest to you. Go to the British Museum and copy the best silhouettes that you can find on the Greek vases.

OUTLINE FOR GUIDED DISCOVERY TECHNIQUE

The Warm-up. The most important rule to remember when setting up a Guided Discovery tour outline is that the focus is on the process of discovery rather than on that of attaining objectives. Guides are not sending people out into the museum to find answers to questions. Guides present problems which have many possible solutions. When planning the opening remarks, tasks are presented before objectives are mentioned. Furthermore, objectives are not emphasized throughout the tour. (Note: this procedure differs from the Inquiry-Discussion technique where objectives are mentioned frequently throughout the tour.)

Directions should be explicit, and they should be given to the entire group before any activities begin. Directions should be as simple as possible, clearly stated (on activity sheets, if applicable), and repeated if necessary. Time should be allowed for questions to ensure that directions are clear. It helps to preface announcing the directions with a request that everyone listen to **all** the directions before leaving for exploration. The number of directions should be kept to a minimum, because too many directions at the beginning of a tour may cause visitors to forget some of them and rush through activities too quickly. If possible, guides might give directions for the first half of the tour, call the group together for a review and additional instructions, and then, have them resume their projects. It should be emphasized to the group that there are no "right" answers and that the tasks are not difficult.

During the warm-up time, guides should comment about the procedures of the museum regarding noise, touching, and other matters of conduct that may be important. Visitors will usually respond favorably when given reasonable explanations. Directions for the group to come together again must be given before they disperse, particularly if the tour is a school group.

Objectives and Learning Goals. In the Discovery method of touring, guides allow visitors to follow their own internal prompts. During the Discovery time, guides can supervise, answer questions, give assistance, and above all, encourage visitors to feel especially comfortable asking questions. Guides may suggest alternative strategies for making new discoveries, and they should try to ensure that there are "real" end results to the process.

Guides must stay in control of the tour, even though people are working independently or in small groups. The role of the interpreters is to encourage, stimulate, and support all responses and conclusions. They provide direction for the tour. They must take into account individual differences and remember that divergent ideas will emerge. Stimulation can be provided by both guides and visitors, as visitors may move from one idea to another on their own. The tour should not become competitive, for when answers becomes more important than looking at the exhibit and contemplating possibilities, learning diminishes. Guided Discovery is most successful when visitors understand what they are seeing and are able to use the information after the tour is over, either in the museum or elsewhere; success follows when people discover knowledge that is meaningful to them as individuals.

Learning goals should include objects and exhibits that share important similarities. Learning theorists maintain that people "discover" effectively when they are picking out common elements. For example, small children might notice that several paintings use the same bright yellow; adults might observe that the furniture in an exhibit is made by hand, or that the Native American's environment influenced design and form of baskets and pottery.

Another example would be to have guides ask visitors to identify specific decorative arts of Native Americans and to understand the objects in the context of their society. (Guides should make sure the given subject is relevant to the particular group.) Visitors would be instructed where specific items are located, i.e., baskets, pots, clothing, tools, religious and ceremonial items, shelter, etc. Visitors should be aware of the guides' expectations at the end of the tour.

The manner in which guides present learning goals makes the difference in whether they challenge or intimidate visitors. Guides should set up the Guided Discovery tour by posing a solvable problem, or presenting a challenge to find comparable characteristics among different objects. The task is more than simple data-retrieval. Visitors must contribute from their observations, experiences, and what they know to be true, in order to draw conclusions. All activities should be focused on the general objectives and the learning goals.

Discovery activity time may be divided into two or more segments. The group might come together periodically for discussion and new directions. Guides may observe group responses at these times for the purpose of assessing progress. If the Guided Discovery objectives are relatively general, and they may be reached through a variety of individual choices, the group may move freely for a relatively long period of time, coming together only for summary discussion. In living history museums, for example, a broad objective such as "to understand how the tasks of living were divided among the family" may be achieved without too much structure. Group members will acquire a wide range of observations that they may contribute to the discussion. Or guides may allow for individual differences by providing alternative learning goals within the broad objectives. If the visitors are a school group, the teacher can assist with the selection of the goals.

Guides often have a tendency to give visitors what seems to them like mini-tests. These are situations in which visitors feel that they have to search for "right" answers. However, guides should set up situations in which there are a number of possible solutions, which enable visitors to diverge from initial premises at any time. The following ideas suggest ways learning goals may be structured to produce a variety of answers.

A. Science, natural history museums
   1. Features common to many creatures.
      a. skin, fur, shell, quills, feathers, scales; look for similarities (protection etc.) how is it useful, contrasts, and so forth.
      b. other ways animals are similar: skeletal, habitat, evolution, and so forth.
   2. Ways of communicating in society.
      a. speaking, body language, telephone, radio, literature, music.
   3. Characteristics common to several objects in the museum.

B. History museums or sites
   1. Concord (Massachusetts) bridge of Revolutionary War fame: the environment, placement of soldiers, the reaction of the townspeople, gathering on the village green, historic houses and their families, patriotism.
   2. What is the same (or different) about the site now and then.

C. Art Museums
   1. portraits: the culture of the time, social class, motivation of artist, opinions about people depicted.
   2. landscapes: as subject, attitudes toward romantic landscapes, American 19th century landscapes related to today's landscapes.

D. Art Museums—abstract art for children
   1. search for similar shapes; discussion of commonality; search for colors. Discussion of why particular colors are used.
   2. Search for similarities among pictures by same artist, recognition of style.

Activities organized to help attain the objectives may differ with each individual or team, depending upon how they choose to work with the problem. Everyone should become actively involved. Visitors can use several methods to record their observations and conclusions. To use an objective mentioned previously (to identify specific decorative arts of the Native American), visitors can take polaroid pictures of a variety of baskets, pots, rugs, and body ornamentation. They may make tape recordings of their comments or conclusions, take notes of ideas and correlations, or draw different decorative elements of baskets or pottery. The materials can be used in the concluding discussion or, if students make up the tour group, taken to the classroom for further investigation.

Conclusion. When the discovery group has reassembled, adequate time should be allowed for sharing discoveries and summarizing findings.

This is also the time for guides to introduce additional information, answer questions, suggest ideas, and perhaps restate the general objectives. All this will require more time than will the Inquiry-Discussion summary, and should be considered when planning tour time. Children particularly enjoy telling their own versions of the Guided Discovery experience, and if possible, each member of the group should have opportunity to tell something about their tour experience. For example, guides might ask if visitors discovered something they did not know before, something special that was meaningful to them, or something about how things related to one another in a new way. Members of the group can also ask questions of one another.

The late Frank Oppenheimer, of the San Francisco Exploratorium, described museum learning by discovery at the 1982 Annual Meeting of the American Association of Museums (1982) as follows:

> *Many people who talk about the discovery method of teaching are really talking about arranging a lesson or an experiment so that students discover what they are supposed to discover. . . . The fullest aspect of discovery whether in a painting, a diorama or a science experiment occurs when each separate piece of the museum is so rich that it has components nobody knew were there (p. 43).*

OTHER TOUR TECHNIQUES

LECTURE

The pure lecture presentation may be necessary at times, but it is not ideal. The guide does most of the talking and attempts to involve visitors through questions are infrequent. This uni-directional format can become tedious and uninteresting. However, docents can develop successful lecturing skills. It is possible to deliver an organized, entertaining, informative lecture. The Lecture technique, however, is not considered ideal for museum touring for any group, unless the audience is highly motivated to learn about the topic and can be expected to listen attentively to the speaker. Lecture tours work best with adult groups. When an audience turns out to be wholly unresponsive, another method may have to be substituted. A lecture is extremely ineffective for audiences whose members are under the age of fifteen.

Experience in museum education reveals that adults generally expect facts to be provided in a lecture situation. Many adults, nonetheless, are willing to answer questions and engage in short discussions. A study conducted at the California Palace of the Legion of Honor compared the effectiveness of the lecture method with the Inquiry-Discussion method. The findings suggest that adult groups responded to both methods, with the guide's knowledge and style of presentation a major factor in the visitors' enjoyment of the tour. The researchers distinguished between the two methods as follows:

> *Lecture is a method for giving a tour in which the docent gives an oral presentation of facts about selected objects in the museum galleries. The inquiry-discussion method . . . is a museum tour in which the visitor's own observations become a means for discovering ideas and relationships about the object. The docent becomes the questioner, intermittently giving background information or illuminating facts and involving the groups of visitors in a discussion (Horn, 1979, p. 2).*

Most visitors will not stand and listen to a lecture tour that fails to interest them. Obviously, they joined the group initially to obtain some information; if the information is not interesting, badly presented, or not forthcoming, the visitors will simply stop listening. They may not leave, however, because some people feel it would be rude to walk away from a tour.

GUIDED INVOLVEMENT.

This technique is similar to Guided Discovery. However, it is highly structured because it is most suitable for very young children or other groups which require continuously structured activities. The group may work together in a single group, or in very small, supervised groups of six to eight persons. Children usually stay in limited areas with adult supervisors. Each activity takes place over a short period of time. Group members respond to their discoveries immediately by talking about them or demonstrating them to the guides or other adults. Preschool groups enjoy looking for a specific color or shape in a painting, or finding something that is common to several items in an exhibit. For example, in a historical museum, visitors might be expected to find things that would be used when eating a meal; to determine how to get a message to a parent today, and to analyze how a message would be sent 100 years from now. These activities should be structured with simple objectives.

RANDOM

This technique constitutes a walk with a guide. It is not a guided tour and little interpretation occurs. Sometimes museums require a guided walk-through. Under most conditions, however, a walk-through requires no leader; written information or other instructions serve to guide visitors' tours. On occasion, groups visiting a museum might request a personal introduction to the collection, but no additional interpretation. Tour guides must not think that they are interpreting a collection by walking around and pointing out the "Navajo rug" or the "Rembrandt."

The random category includes school groups (especially high school groups) which refuse to listen or participate. They may have been told to remain together, and frustrated guides may find it expedient to walk along with them, speaking in generalities. This is not learning, interpretation, or fun; it is crowd control.

QUESTIONING STRATEGIES

The museum visit is enhanced when visitors observe objects in the manner professionals do in their respective disciplines. For example, botanists, art critics, historians, archaeologists, carpenters, potters, geologists, and so forth, focus on technical or aesthetic aspects of objects which may add to their store of knowledge. Questions to visitors are a way in which their attention can be directed to the same specific details. Visitors can learn more easily about objects if they start with the features that they believe make the object special or unique. Details of objects must be noted before differences or similarities can be discussed. Questions can encourage thinking about the objects and help in relating prior knowledge to the understanding of new information. Questions invite thinking, comparing, and evaluating, and all of these thought processes contribute to understanding.

Visitors may understand the meaning of words used in questions differently from the way guides use them. Unfortunately, terms that describe the qualities of objects also may differ in meaning from one discipline to another. For example, "weight" usually refers to actual heaviness of an object, but "visual weight" in works of art refers to a nonphysical quality. Geologic time is different in the abstract than in daily time, especially for children. Even daily time and past time may involve different terms. Time periods have a variety of meanings for children at different ages (Vukelich, 1984). Guides thus must be aware that special terms are used by different disciplines, and visitors may not understand them.

Visitors often respond silently to questions. They may not share their thoughts. When they were in school, teaching often focused upon facts and correct responses. With this kind of classroom environment as background for their learning, museum visitors may be reluctant to answer questions out loud because they are not sure of the "right" answers. Guides should be aware of visitors' general reluctance to respond in public and to "being wrong." Guides should also avoid questions that may interfere with group participation. However, visitors can be asked questions and can be asked to give answers in ways that will establish an atmosphere of relaxed, open discussion. For example, instead of asking what the group sees, a series of questions that direct attention to specific attributes will put visitors at ease and encourage responses. Replies are encouraged to questions that ask for a specific color, shape, comparative size, structure, or aspect of identification. Questions need to be precise enough so that visitors will know what to look for. To ask a tour group to identify design in a textile exhibit will elicit a variety of answers associated with fabric pattern, symbolism, and cut and style of clothing.

To establish clarity, however, design could be defined initially by pointing out specific types of design in particular textiles, and then, visitors might be asked to look for similar designs in related museum objects. Occasionally, guides might provide information that offers background for questions. Visitors usually look more carefully at exhibits after being assisted in developing meaningful perceptions of one or more objects.

Guides may fall into the trap of asking irrelevant questions if they fail to acquire a sense of what students or visitors know already. However, the problem of irrelevance can be avoided by proposing the unexpected or altering a fact to trigger an unusual response. Students can be asked what they would find if they climbed into a painting and chose an object, or in the case of abstract work, a color to "take out" with them. If an adult were to go back in time (appropriate for an historic site), what would be important to them to find out from the people of the town? What important twentieth century discovery would impact upon an eighteenth or nineteenth century person?

TYPES OF QUESTIONS

Questions can be generally classified as:

1. memory
2. convergent
3. divergent
4. judgemental

In each of these categories, questions can be concrete or abstract. Concrete questions are about facts and concepts that can be defined, identified, or seen. Abstract questions and answers relate to ideas, values, expressions of feeling, interpretations of events, and so forth. Patriotism, religious beliefs, democracy, tyranny, duty, and love, are abstractions that are understood either through experience or by example. Abstractions are more difficult for guides to interpret, especially for children who may lack both experience and cognitive capacity for dealing with them. Although questions may be ordered from concrete to abstract, they may also be categorized on the basis of function. The different types of question can be used during tours to encourage observation, knowledge recall, and foster imaginative ways of thinking about objects and relating ideas to them.

1. Memory questions—these relate directly to what is seen—facts, names of things, precise recall, exact definitions of objects or events. Memory questions are concrete and the easiest to formulate. There is usually only one right answer. Such questions may be prefaced by the words "how many . . . ," "what is the . . . ," "name the . . . ," "which one . . . ."
2. Convergent questions—these seek the most appropriate answer or the best answer. They focus on specifics. Convergent questions and answers zero in on what visitors already know or perceive. Although

people may suggest different answers to questions, each question has one best answer.

3. Divergent questions—these encourage multiple answers. They are sometimes called "open-ended" questions because visitors are encouraged to think of many possibilities. The questions may be prefaced by "what if . . . ," "how many ways . . . ," "imagine that . . . ." These questions demand imaginative thinking and exploration of all facets of an issue. They do not encourage the one "right" or most appropriate answer.
4. Judgemental questions—these stimulate each visitor to evaluate and to choose, that is, to formulate an opinion, value, or belief that is personal, and perhaps, unique.

LEVELS OF QUESTIONS

As children grow and learn, they are able to draw upon more and more complex ways of thinking. Tour questions for different age groups should be presented in a sequence that parallels the development of young people from direct perception and concrete understanding to abstract reasoning. Questions also should lead from simple to complex in steps that will assist older visitors in discovering objects by naming, discriminating, classifying, making inferences, and evaluating.

NAMING OBJECTS

As visitors relate new information to the objects, guides must define and restate names of objects and specialized vocabulary words during the tour. Many visitors will lack sufficient background information for understanding strange names or words. They may encounter many unknown objects and ideas in museums, and without being condescending, guides should both explain why objects in the tour have unusual names and define unusual or technical words. Questions pertaining to names would correspond to the "memory" type of question.

DISCRIMINATING CHARACTERISTICS OF OBJECTS AND EVENTS

To experience any object fully, its particular characteristics must be observed. For example, differentiating bright from dull, big from small, elegant from crude, rough from smooth, or useful from decorative, requires discrimination. Although visitors usually are aware of details, they may not distinguish among the fine characteristics of familiar objects. Perception is often gross; identification is made by naming objects by their obvious rather than by their unique qualities. For example, when looking at an object, many visitors think only about the idea or subject it represents; they neglect details of color, texture, composition, and balance. In the same way, a restored Colonial room will be viewed as a whole until its furniture, wallpaper, fabrics, and so on, are noticed individually.

"The physical characteristics of objects need to be observed and discriminated with systematic thoroughness, using all the externally oriented senses" (Gagne, 1965, p. 183). Interpreters should lead visitors through the challenge of distinguishing characteristics of objects before they move them into more complex ideas related to history, cultural context, and so on. This practice encourages every visitor to notice the same aspects of the object at the same time. Discriminating questions are usually concrete and call for specific answers. These questions would be the "convergent" type.

CLASSIFYING AND GROUPING OBJECTS AND EVENTS

Questions which assist people in classifying and grouping objects fall in the "convergent" category. Classification is accomplished on the basis of common elements among the objects. These elements include position (above and below), direction (horizontal, vertical), shape (square, triangle, etc.), size (large, small), weight (heavy, light), time (minute, day, hour, year, century, past, present, future), force (push, pull), and volume. They may be used to classify many different kinds of objects. Objects may be classified in more than one way, too. For example, animals, plants, or works of art can all be classified according to appearance (hairy, alternating leaves, oil painting) and also according to function (carnivorous, deciduous, portrait).

Visitors can be directed to take note of the organization of designs or composition in art, growth patterns in nature, identifying characteristics of rock strata and crystal structures, by comparing, contrasting, and studying relationships between similar objects. Such analyses are not necessarily available to children. "Jean Piaget once wrote that learning a concept takes place only to the degree to which it is reinvented" (Samples, 1976, p. 102). Such reinvention, or discovering something for oneself, is based on the ability to classify. When visitors learn to identify unique qualities in objects, and thus, discover new ways of grouping them, they also acquire new knowledge. For example, after noticing the characteristics of succulent plants and classifying several of them, interpreters could ask visitors to look for another succulent plant with characteristics similar to those observed; the exercise encourages visitors to practice their skills in discrimination and classification.

MAKING INFERENCES

When visitors are able to identify, name, discriminate, and classify objects, they should also be able to discuss them and to propose questions about their characteristics. It is at this stage of questioning that historical connections should be discussed. The ways in which people work, travel, receive instruction, keep records and documents, create things, use ornamentation, hold religious beliefs, organize governments or structure societies, are among the many cultural factors that might be used to connect objects to contemporary life. Open-ended questions, which are useful in exploring inferences, have more than one answer. "What if . . . ," "how would it be if . . . ," "imagine . . . " are some questioning techniques tour guides might use to encourage visitors to make inferences based on what they know.

Creative thinking is encouraged through questions that invite visitors to express their own ideas. The highest level of human thought is conceptual and insightful. Such abstract thinking depends on prior knowledge, and it often seizes on an unexpected combination of previously unrelated concepts and principles. The process of drawing insights together is an important part of inferential thinking and learning. Unfortunately, it is often devalued in school classrooms in favor of task completion exercises and expressing "right" answers. In the museum setting, however, visitors' imaginations can be stimulated. For example, in an anthropology museum, visitors might be asked what could be done with a particular plant—eat the fruit, weave the stems or vines into baskets, use parts for soap, use the fibers for thread, dye, and so forth.

EVALUATION & JUDGEMENT

Evaluation processes also offer opportunities for complex analyses. Visitors have to develop reasons in support of their viewpoints. The notions used in evaluation questions include: choose, decide, evaluate, judge, assess, give your opinion, tell which is preferable. These correspond, of course, to "judgemental" type questions.

WAITING FOR ANSWERS

Another important aspect of dealing with questions is centered on the amount of time guides should wait for visitor responses. Visitors not only look at interesting or unusual objects, they also think about them, formulate ideas, make connections, listen to guides, and attend to the discussion. Some of them will be responsive to what a guide is saying; others will be distracted and inattentive. Therefore, guides should be conscious of individual differences in reactions of visitors to presentations. Guides should be prepared to interact with them at all levels of responsiveness.

A wait of at least five to six seconds after asking a question gives a visitor sufficient time to formulate a reply. Open-ended questions, or those that are concerned with more complex information may require ten to fifteen seconds for a response. Wait-time also makes clear that an answer is expected. Waiting may seem difficult to guides at first, but it establishes an informal, unhurried attitude that is important in establishing the tone of tours. If, after the wait-time, there are no responses, guides might consider restating the question, explaining the subject again, giving another definition, or using different words. It is always possible that the visitors either did not understand the first question clearly, or did not feel sufficiently comfortable to reply.

Several questions, or variations of the same question, should not be asked in rapid succession. Sometimes guides rephrase them so quickly that visitors cannot keep up with them. Asking questions rapidly implies that no response is expected, because no one has time to speak. Silence can generate positive rapport—visitors need some quiet pauses during the tours. Guides who talk continuously may unknowingly discourage comments or fail to provide visitors with time to contemplate.

ENCOURAGING VISITORS' QUESTIONS

Good touring allows visitors time to ask questions of interpreters. By means of visitors' questions, guides determine the level at which they can provide information. Studies of visitor comments during tours reveal that "many adults as well as children behave as if they are following unwritten rules that inhibit asking questions" (Marsh, 1983, p. 18). These "rules" include fears that asking questions (1) is not polite, (2) may be embarrassing to the other person, (3) may expose ignorance, (4) will challenge the person in authority, (5) may invite ridicule, and (6) may waste the guide's time. However, visitor questions reveal how much of the exhibit they understand. Frequently, questions appear to be superficial, (inquiring about how much something is worth), but they may initiate discussion of background information. Guides also can move readily from these questions into discussions that are concerned with learning goals and objectives.

In every way possible, guides should promote the belief among visitors that all questions and answers are worthy of consideration and will be treated respectfully. However, when guides ask for factual information visitors may be embarrassed when they do not know the answer. Sometimes when students fail to remember facts, teachers become embarrassed and chastise students publicly for forgetting. It is better, therefore, to provide facts and to ask visitors to make comparisons, contrasts, and inferences about information. When visitor responses seem too far removed from the subject matter, guides can respond constructively with comments that steer them back on target. When responses are consistently different than expected, perhaps the questions are not worded properly and need to be rephrased carefully. Pursuing an answer until the right one is found is awkward for everyone. If the same members of the group respond repeatedly, preventing others from participating, their answers can be accepted, and questions can be directed toward other individuals, from whom additional information can be requested. Encouraging visitor interaction in the museum setting promotes both positive attitudes toward the museum and its exhibits and new learning experiences.

TOUR AIDS

Occasionally Lecture-Discussion, Inquiry-Discussion, or Guided Discovery interpretive techniques can be combined. For all visitors, guides can use games, improvisation, hands-on materials (real or facsimile), storytelling, audio-visual programs, and available interactive exhibits. The activities will vary, of course, with the characteristics of the group. But they should should support the tour objectives. They must be used appropriately and with forethought. Improvisation, imagination, and perception games are not meaningful in every situation. Lying down on the floor and "being red," or pretending to be in another time may not always be fun.

GAMES

These activities are most appropriate for the young school group or family group. They should, of necessity, be of short duration and have some specific purpose in the tour. A game can be either a warm-up activity or a means of fulfilling a learning goal. For the very young, Guided Discovery techniques can be introduced as games. They can be carried out by individuals, small groups, or teams of two persons. For example, small children might select an object or exhibit they like or dislike, and then provide reasons why. Or, they might be asked to notice two or three different and unique things about an object. Perception games in art museums can use color cards, cut-out shapes, or objects perceived via the senses. However, games can easily become competitive; when children become more intent on being "first" than on learning, they do not select answers carefully or think them through. The best games focus on divergent problems with no right answers. Games should be used to support tours; they are not substitutes for tours.

IMPROVISATION

Children and adults often enjoy acting out situations presented to them. Interpreters with skills at leading improvisations will find that they can use them to good advantage. This technique is used in creative dramatics, and it can be quite successful in the museum setting. Improvisation is useful for brief periods, with any number of participants. However, it should be relevant to the tour objectives. Role-playing, pretending to live in another time or culture, dressing-up in costumes, and using objects for improvisation can be very effective for certain groups. Guides should practice giving directions for such activities. They must be clear, concise, and allow for multiple variations on the theme of the improvisation. Encouragement and support by guides and other group members are keys to success, along with group or team planning. If not done properly, children and adults can become embarrassed and uncomfortable during improvisations.

HANDS-ON MATERIALS

Many museums and historical sites today use materials and objects, which people can handle, to illustrate tour learning goals. The materials can be real objects or facsimiles, and they can be aids in helping people understand objectives. As exhibit materials are often fragile and cannot be touched, hands-on components constitute satisfactory substitutes for making exhibits come alive. Many museums use baskets, bags, or carts of materials to illustrate important aspects of museum collections. Samples of fired clay, etching plates, photographs, leaves, geological samples, shells, fabrics, and examples of art media are only a few possibilities for hands-on materials. Some zoological parks, science, and natural history museums permit visitors to touch snakes. The feel of a snake's cool, dry skin is an unusual experience, and it helps calm unreasonable fears of snakes. Any unusual creatures, as well as machines, artifacts, or facsimile objects are exciting to touch and will be eagerly approached by young and old alike. Specimens should be made available, even if they are somewhat inferior in quality. Maps, posters, and diagrams may be placed in the gallery prior to the tour for use at the appropriate time. It saves time to have several samples of an object when it is to be passed around.

PROJECT-DIRECTED AND DATA RETRIEVAL

Certain activities can be used to accomplish a specific task. An example of a fairly recent project-directed activity is the development of data-retrieval sheets. Students are asked to find answers to questions about listed subjects and to record them. This is a particularly good activity for school children, even though it could interfere with the Guided Discovery technique because it is so structured. Again, competition among school children can be a problem unless there are several different projects for the group. Project-directed activities will be more effective when teachers and guides collaborate on them.

STORYTELLING

Anecdotes and stories can enliven tours and illustrate important ideas. Effective storytellers are also performers, and their reward is attentive audiences. Folktales, myths, and historical stories need to be told enthusiastically with gestures and expressions. They should be chosen to illustrate or emphasize tour objectives. Visitors can participate in the story by answering questions about it and contributing ideas to it. Guides can research stories or create original tales from background information about the objects or exhibits. Group storytelling is another possibility, with members taking turns contributing to the story. However, some anecdotes are meaningful only if the storyteller knows visitor characteristics. For children, it may be helpful to recap the important elements of the story and make tour connections obvious. This can be done by asking specific questions that lead to the right answer. Any age group will find folk tales, poetry, and children's books to be valuable sources of cultural insight.

AUDIO-VISUAL AIDS

Tape-recorders, slides, videotapes, and films represent teaching aids that can be used in museums. Many museums have special rooms for presentations, but smaller museums may use audiovisual equipment only in their galleries, either temporarily or permanently. Tape recorders can supplement exhibits with authentic sounds of nature or animals, music from the period or culture, and special settings for storytelling and other activities. To be effective, the length of time media aids are on should be planned and controlled. They should be introduced at only appropriate times during a tour.

Portable slide projectors with self-contained viewing screens and tape recorders with speakers are useful for presenting slides in galleries. Viewing slides presents additional visual information about objects, different cultures, historical sites, nature, and geography. When slides are carefully chosen for a specific purpose, they can be effective tour aides. They provide breadth to the attainment of tour objectives by providing information about objects and their environments in novel ways, thus offering variety to the presentation. The screen must be in a slightly darkened area for everyone to see well. Individual slides should be projected only briefly—only as long as necessary for visitors to see them and to acquire information about them.

Video cassette players can also be placed in galleries. Many major exhibitions have supplemental video tapes that provide invaluable visual information. When used with tour groups, the program length should be considered. The age and type of audience is important when guides use video programs as part of the tour; vocabulary and information may not be appropriate for young people.

FILMS

Showing films requires the same considerations as video tapes, but requirements for space, darker rooms, and perhaps a projectionist are more stringent. It is possible to set up the equipment in a museum gallery; however, the significance of the film versus the museum experience with its exhibits and objects should be considered. There are excellent films that present ancient legends and myths, animated explanations of scientific and mathematical problems, art history supplements, and so on. School districts, universities, and libraries are possible resources for excellent films, as commercial rental fees are relatively high. All equipment should be made ready to operate in advance of the tour, and it should be checked to make sure that the film is threaded properly, bulbs are working, and sound is adjusted.

INTERACTIVE EXHIBITS

If there are working exhibits or hands-on activities for the general public, guides can either include these experiences as part of the tour, or announce that visitors can return to them after the tour. If included in the tour, time must be allowed for each person to participate.

SUPPLEMENTAL TOUR INFORMATION

PRETOUR PREPARATION

Interpreters should check into the volunteer office at the museum early enough to determine whether recent changes in the tour or in the exhibitions have occurred, put on an identifying tag or label, and review the tour outline to be used. Interpreters must have time to bring all the elements together for a successful tour. Arriving only a few minutes before the group is due is not conducive to a relaxed, calm state of mind.

KNOW THE MUSEUM

Training in facts about the museum should be part of the volunteer training process. When it is not, guides can easily research for themselves the most frequently asked questions. Samples of such questions include:

1. Where are the locations of telephones, drinking fountains, and restrooms?
2. What are staff responsibilities?
3. How did the museum begin?
4. What are the sources of the collections?
5. What are the funding sources of the museum?
6. What are the available programs?
7. Who are the local support groups?
8. What are the museum's volunteer needs?
9. What are the membership fees and benefits?

ARRANGING TIME WITHIN THE TOUR

Guides using Inquiry-Discussion or Guided Discovery techniques must allow more "open," unstructured time for exploration, group discussion, and sharing. If one object or area generates a great deal of interest and interaction, guides should be prepared to allow for it, perhaps by planning to eliminate other objects. If the group fails to respond as enthusiastically as expected, introducing more inquiry or guided discovery activities may stimulate discussion.

Other factors important in planning time for the tour include allowing time for removing coats, group introductions, dividing large groups among several guides, and moving groups between galleries. Guides should gauge in advance the time required to walk between galleries and add one or two minutes for the transition. It takes a little longer for groups than individuals to walk together, arrive at a destination, and refocus attention. A few minutes should be allowed for visitors to look at things along the way, even without stopping, and to orient themselves to the new surroundings.

The "warm-up" time at the beginning of a tour and the "wrap-up" or summary at the end of it are crucial to its success. A minimum of five minutes for each activity should be allowed. As guides become accustomed to using the Inquiry-Discussion and Guided Discovery techniques, more time may be allocated for summary of the tour.

It is essential that guides be aware of the exact time throughout the tour so as not to foreshorten the summary period. Even if the time allowed for the entire tour is flexible, guides should remember that attention spans vary within groups. Estimates of actual time for successful group talking and looking is 45 minutes. For most children under eight years, 25 to 30 minutes is sufficient. These are generalities, as some groups whose members are highly motivated and responsive may enjoy longer tours. However, one hour is usually the maximum length of time that should be allocated for adult tours. If individual activities, or guided discovery techniques are used, perhaps more time may be allowed.

WAITING FOR THE GROUP'S ARRIVAL

Museums should have a policy regarding how to deal with late tour groups. Volunteer guides are often left waiting at the door by groups who fail to cancel. If the daily schedule is filled, a late group can disrupt all those that follow. A policy in frequent use in museums states that guides are not required to conduct a tour if the group is twenty minutes late—unless the tour leader calls the museum and new arrangements are made. Late groups may have to accept shorter tours, but they should be informed ahead of time that this is a possibility if they arrive late.

Names and phone numbers for scheduled tour group leaders, in case of delay or confusion about dates, should be available for every tour. The museum office should also have a policy of informing tour groups in advance that guides conduct tours only by appointment. The public may assume erroneously that tours will be conducted at any time by paid staff.

ESTABLISHING RAPPORT WITH THE GROUP

If the entire group is approached in a friendly manner, with sincere interest, rapport is relatively easily established. A smile, relaxed posture, and air of confidence in one's ability to lead are personal characeristics that can be practiced and mastered. Good interaction with the group is the first priority of touring.

In addition to guides giving visitor groups the names by which they wish to be addressed, brief personal statements also help set an informal tone. Guides might mention how long they have been guiding tours and the particular interests they have in the exhibits. Special information about what visitors are allowed to touch should also be in the introduction. Visitors need to be cautioned before the tour so that they will not be embarrassed later. Occasionally an alarm system is designed so that leaning over roped-off areas to examine objects will set it off. Even adults may fail to understand that objects and exhibits may be irreplaceable and should not be touched. They do not realize that constant touching damages fabric, canvas and paint, and wears away wood, stone, and bone. A good example of wear is a statue in St. Peter's Cathedral in Rome. The marble foot of the sculpture has been touched so often over the centuries that the toes have worn down. Also, many visitors may think that objects on display are not originals, and therefore, are replaceable.

Before the tour begins, the exact route through the museum should be described. Background information about the museum may be given at this point, or, if more appropriate, during the tour. Adults accompanying school groups should be given special instructions at this time. Teachers and parents with large student groups may need to take responsibility for discipline or directing the students.

TOUR LOGISTICS

On a tour everyone within a group must be able to see, hear, and move easily from one location to another. Various methods may be planned in advance, based on the size and age of the group. Teachers can help with the organization. For example, young children like to walk in pairs with friends. Older children may resent regimentation, but they will follow in an unstructured group. High school and adult groups tend to be more independent and often separate as they are moved about on the tour. If the museum requires that groups stay together, or if there are large numbers of visitors that need supervision, guides should announce tour requirements at the outset. In situations where there are many people around, members of the tour group may have trouble hearing unless they stay close to the guide.

MOVING GROUPS AROUND

Moving several tour groups at one time through a museum depends entirely upon museum size and layout. If groups move at a steady pace, most museums are large enough to handle groups in each gallery or hall. A smaller museum will require that guides prepare ahead of time for handling groups of different sizes. Large groups, such as a school bus of about 70 students, should be broken into smaller groups. A good ratio is fifteen visitors to one guide; twenty-five to one is the maximum size possible for satisfactory interaction and discussion. Several small groups can tour in various areas of the museum at the same time and move in a preplanned way so as not to interfere with each other. A volunteer can also act as "timekeeper" and signal when it is time to move on. Some museums prefer that guides stand in one area throughout the tour and receive each group. This may be the least effective tour for school groups because there is no time to establish rapport with the groups and to discuss object connections. Also, repeating the same "routine" over and over becomes tedious.

When a tour group is moving from one area to another, it is helpful to highlight specific objects to be looked for in the next area. Preparation before the group moves on sets up expectations and provides continuity and impetus to the tour. Younger students could be asked to form a double line and follow the guide to the next area. If no organization is followed, a small "mob" forms that may crowd, push, or lag behind, especially in narrow hallways and stairs. Some examples for giving moving instructions to children include:

1. Directions for getting organized and to wait for the next directive: "Please find a partner and stand in line in front of me."
2. Directions to anticipate something and a place to go: "When we reach the next gallery, look for the (smallest animal, dollhouse, spinning wheel, painting of the dragon, bright red flowers, etc.) and stand there together."
3. Directions for behavior while moving: "Follow me quietly so that we do not disturb others in the museum."

Moving adult groups may be more difficult. As with children, developing anticipation of the next gallery is important for maintaining interest, because many adults want to remain in the gallery in which they find themselves in order to look at things more closely. Once an adult group is dispersed, it is difficult to bring them back together. Adults tend to talk to each other, read labels, and become distracted. Guides frequently find adult groups diminish in size with every move to another area, except for large, outdoor museums where the exhibits are spaced farther apart and the tour group must stay together to get from one point to another. Special interest groups who request lectures or tours probably will be the most attentive of all groups.

An announcement of intentions at the beginning of a tour lets people know what to expect, whether the tour will be brief, how it will move through gallery A, B, and C, and how much time will be allowed to look individually at exhibits at the conclusion of the tour. If the tour technique is to be a lecture, it is best to have chairs or benches available for adults. Standing in one place for more than ten minutes can be uncomfortable for most and impossible for some adult visitors. Moving about the gallery, even a little, helps relieve "museum legs" and keeps visitors interested in the tour. No Lecture-Discussion tour should be longer than thirty to forty minutes. Inquiry-Discussion tours, which actively involve visitors in looking and talking, should not exceed forty-five minutes. A Guided Discovery tour, or tours using hands-on activities, may be an hour in length. If there are a few individuals who really want more information, guides might continue with smaller groups after the main tour is over.

LARGE GROUPS: DIVIDE AND CONQUER

Large groups may arrive with from fifty to four hundred visitors.

It is wise to control the maximum size for tour groups wherever space is a problem. However, very large groups usually visit a museum for an introductory tour rather than a structured tour. Guides can provide a brief welcome to the entire group, which is followed by additional general information and structured tours for those who seek them. A warm welcome of visitors, and consideration of their needs, makes a significant impression. Many visitors never develop rapport with tour guides, and thus, they become less interested in looking, reading information, and taking self-guided tours.

When large numbers of visitors choose the guided tour, guides should try to divide them into small groups in order to enable each visitor to see, hear, and move about easily. In some unplanned circumstances, one guide may have to work with a group of fifty or more visitors. Outdoor museums usually prepare for this situation by providing benches and predetermined locations for talks. Indoor museums cannot handle such large tour groups easily, and guides must do the best they can. The primary difficulty with speaking to large groups is that those in the back cannot hear; therefore, discussion takes place only among those in the front. Persons in the back either try to move within hearing distance, or break away from the group and wander about alone. A portable microphone should be considered when large groups are frequent. After a brief, traveling tour of the museum, a large group may be dispersed to tour independently.

TOUR PROBLEMS

INFORMATION OVERLOAD

Groups should not be given too much information in one tour. Artifacts and historic sites have strong visual presences that have to be absorbed by visitors. Many lack the powers of concentration necessary to listen attentively to facts while trying to examine an object, especially if it is highly complex or unfamiliar. However, there should be adequate and appropriate information available for visitors, which will enable them to interpret what they see. Information can be presented in both written and verbal forms.

OTHER VISITORS

When uninvited visitors join a tour, it becomes a problem if the group has scheduled the tour or has paid for it. Other visitors sometimes crowd out the original tour members, who resent the intrusion, especially when it is difficult to see and hear. Guides are expected to be in charge of such disturbances. The "joiners" may not realize that the tour was prearranged and is not open to the general public. Guides should explain that other tour guides are available. If the group is small enough, joiners can be invited to listen at the back; if the group is too large, they can be asked to join the next public tour. If the tour is already a public tour, everyone will have to be accepted.

THE RESTLESS FRINGE

In many tours there are those who hover at the edge of the group as if they want to dart away at any moment. Adults often drift in and out of tours, but school groups usually stay together, unless instructed otherwise. The students who appear inattentive need to be included in the discussion—those in the back of the group may be called on first. Guides can minimize tour restlessness by moving through or around the group while talking. It is tempting to speak only to persons at the front and to ignore the rest of the group when the only responsiveness is from these persons. Tours then become private tours for four or five members of the group, which causes the rest of the audience to drift away.

PROBLEMS WITH STUDENT TOURS

> *I once asked a group of children what they did when they visited a museum. "Nothing," one of the kids replied. "Nothing?" I asked. "Have you ever been to a . . . museum before?" "Yup, we been here before, walked halfway 'round the place. Walk and look. Walk, walk, walk. Look and walk" (Levinson, 1981, p. 14).*

Unfortunately, many students have had the same experience as the child in the illustration above. We hope this is not the most vivid memory of most young people who make field trips to museums. Boredom during a trip, however, can create problems with school groups. It can negate all opportunities for learning.

Scheduling problems occur as a consequence of the hours museums are open, when guides are available, required school class periods, and mandated tests. And sometimes teachers wish to prepare students for the trip, but the museum fails to prepare materials for them.

Discipline Problems. When one or more members of a group are disruptive or talk continuously, guides can ask them to leave the group and wait in some designated place until the tour is over. If they are children, and an adult with the group is available for supervising them, the adult should be asked to remove them from the others. The guide's responsibility is to the larger group, and a few persons should not be allowed to ruin the experience for all. Guides are also responsible for protecting museum property, and any group member who appears to be abusing the museum and its exhibits should be asked to leave. When necessary, an adult member of the group can be sent for a security guard.

Adult discipline problems may also occur. Some adults may be mentally disturbed, and they may behave in unusual ways during public lectures, gallery talks, and tours. They may become abusive or argumentative with guides and other visitors. In mild situations, guides can avoid arguments; they might even ask the disruptive person to leave the tour group if they are affecting the tour.

LACK OF INTEREST

Some groups are in museums only because the tour was planned for them. If it becomes apparent that group members in general have little interest in the tour, guides might quickly shift to another tour technique, or shorten the tour in order to allow time for individuals to tour themselves unguided. Sometimes this is necessary with teenage groups. As small groups of individuals look at objects and talk among themselves, perhaps they can be approached with a few questions. Adolescents prefer to ask questions and to talk to guides in twos and threes. As the discussion continues, other small groups may join, and eventually, perhaps the tour can be resumed.

THE TALKING VISITOR

Some members of adult groups monopolize discussions in a group, excluding the possibility of member participation. Guides should postpone conversations with individuals until the tour is over. Interest diminishes quickly when people are excluded from conversation. Visitors may have questions that need to be answered, but unless they are of interest to others in the group, guides should not discuss them at length during the tour. When visitors seek the attention of the group, other members may find their behavior unacceptable.

INTERFERENCE WITH TOUR GUIDES

Teachers and parents may unknowingly interfere with the field trip and inhibit meaningful tour experiences. While their objectives may be the same—learning and stimulating the students—teachers or parents may attempt to assist in a manner at odds with the technique selected for the tour. They may also try to take over control in the midst of a tour, which often causes disruptions.

Adults can support guides by reinforcing the information presented to the group, assisting with discipline problems, and helping move the group from one area to another. Disruptive behavior by adults with student groups is infrequent, but it does happen. Some teachers may attempt to take over the guides' role, usually unwittingly, and provide information themselves about the museum collection. Guides have to decide how they want to handle these disruptions. Many guides yield to the teacher, feeling that the teacher knows the group best and understands what should be said. Guides might wait until after the first interruption to see whether the teacher's lecture is adequate. Self-confidence, consideration, and good manners will help guides work through difficult situations. Sometimes it may be necessary to ask adults bluntly for their cooperation.

Parents or teachers may ask questions on the basis of their personal interests, thus diverting the group from its tour objectives. Guides might offer to discuss other subjects after the student tour is finished rather than talk to the adults and lose the students' attention altogether. Some adults may challenge the focus of the tour. Guides should state briefly, without apologies, the reasons for choosing the objectives. Presumably, guides have planned the tour in advance, taking into consideration available information about the group; they need not change objectives at this point, especially to satisfy someone's whim. Most situations that come up during the tour are handled best through brief, polite responses. Further explanation may be offered afterwards if necessary. Museum guides should not have to be on the defensive regarding their tour plans.

Some adults who accompany student groups do not participate in the tour, but carry on private conversations with one another, leaving student discipline to the interpreter. They may not be aware that talking distracts both guides and members of the group. When this happens, guides can request that the conversation cease or take place farther away from the group. Guides should make clear to adults before the tour begins that it is the guides' task is to discuss and interpret the exhibits, it is the parents' or teacher's job to discipline if necessary.

ILLNESS

Most museums have security guards on duty to assist with sudden illnesses or accidents. Tour guides should either find help or send someone for a guard in case of emergencies. Visitors who fall should not be allowed to get up quickly. They should be asked to wait for someone trained in first aid in the event they are injured. Unless trained and given specific instructions by the institution to do so, under no circumstances should interpreters become involved in administering first aid.

Tour guides must choose appropriate tour techniques according to the visitor group. Questioning strategies follow a definite pattern, using memory, convergent, divergent and judgemental questions. These lead from simple to complex, and help visitors think more abstractly about objects and exhibits. Tours can also be enhanced by including games, hands-on materials, storytelling, audio-visual aids, and so forth. Preplanning is the best assurance of successful tours.

REFERENCES

Gagne, R. M. (1965). **The Conditions of Learning**. New York: Holt, Rinehart and Winston, Inc.

Horn, A. (1979). The adult tour dilemma. **Roundtable Reports: The Journal of Museum Education. 4**(4), 1-4. Washington, DC: Museum Education Roundtable.

Lessinger, L. & Gillis, D. (1976). **Teaching as A Performing Art.** Dallas: Crescendo Publications, Inc.

Levinson, B. (1981). Playing with film. **Roundtable Reports: The Journal of Museum Education. 6**(1,2), 14.

Marsh, C. (1983). How to encourage museum visitors to ask questions: an experimental investigation. **Roundtable Reports: The Journal of Museum Education. 8**(2), 18-19. Washington, DC: Museum Education Roundtable.

Oppenheimer, F. (1982). Address at the 1982 Annual Meeting of the American Association of Museums, Boston, Massachusetts. Cited in **Museum News, 60,** 36-45. Washington, DC: American Association of Museums.

Samples, R. (1976). **The Metaphoric Mind.** Reading, Massachusetts: Addison-Wesley Publishing Co.

School Council, Museum in Education. (1972). **Pterodactyls and Old Lace.** London: Evans Brothers Ltd. and Methuen Educational Limited.

Vukelich, R. (1984). Time language for interpreting history collections to children. **Museum Studies Journal. 1**(4). 43-50. San Francisco: Center for Museum Studies, John F. Kennedy University.

Whitman, N. A. (1983). **A Handbook for Group Discussion Leaders: Alternatives to Lecturing Medical Students to Death.** Salt Lake City, Utah: University of Utah School of Medicine.

Wittrock, M. C. (1966). The learning by discovery hypothesis. In L. C. Shulman and E. R. Keislar, **Learning by Discovery: A Critical Appraisal.** 33-76. Chicago: Rand McNally & Co.

CHAPTER SIX
Audiences: Who's Listening?

School Age Groups • Mixed Age Groups • The Gifted Student • Young Adults, ages 18 to 30 • The Adult Visitor • Senior Adults • The Family Group • Minorities • The Handicapped • Out-of-Town or Foreign Visitors

Visitors to museums and historic sites are of all ages and have scores of different reasons for being there. Some visitors are travelers who want to see museums and sites in the area. A few are scholars who come to conduct research in their areas of interest. Others who are from school classrooms use museums as learning resources.

Museum visitors have been surveyed and investigated with increasing intensity for several years. We have seen a period during which museums have developed an interest in identifying their audiences, thus enabling them to plan programs and exhibits that better serve the public. All kinds of museums have conducted surveys. One of the earliest studies, that of the National Research Center of the Arts, showed that in 1972 sixty percent of adult art museum visitors attributed their interest in art to the fact that someone in their families took them to museums when they were children. Seventy percent of the visitors were also influenced by friends or teachers. Only three percent of adult art museum visitors, however, credited school trips as being the source of their interest in museums.

These findings indicate, among visitors surveyed, that visits in the company of people they knew well and liked produced memorable excursions whereas school field trips yielded few lasting impressions. Later, a 1981 survey by the American Council for the Arts found that a sizeable percentage of the public is in general disinterested in attending museums. Fifty-three percent felt "there is always pretty much the same thing shown, so there is no need to go very often" (p. 9). Twenty-six percent said they did not feel comfortable going to museums. The conclusions to be drawn from investigations such as these suggest that museums have not been as responsive to their audiences as they might wish.

Unfortunately, most museum audience surveys do not question children, partly because of the poor reliability of their answers. Thus the opinions of school groups, who make up most tours in museums and historical sites, have not been surveyed extensively about their attitudes concerning field trips.

Many types of groups visit museums. For example, school groups are small "cultures" in themselves. The students know each other and their teachers well, and they have worked and studied together for a long period of time. They know what to anticipate from their classmates, and they may have about the same level of preparation when they come to the museum. Other groups could be adults who meet together regularly to pursue a shared interest. Groups may be together temporarily, that is, organized only for the purpose of the tour. Senior citizen centers may provide tours, bringing together people who are strangers to one another. The same is true of tour companies, who offer stops at area museums to tourists or convention groups. In addition, the museum may offer tours to the general public at specific times, bringing together random groupings of visitors of all ages. These "accidental" groups can have similar or different characteristics, which are difficult to predict in advance.

Individuals in any group will be widely variable in their motivations and expectations. Interpreters should expect that some members of groups may anticipate an uninteresting or boring tour. (The person in charge of the group may influence the group attitude.) Foreign visitors are often curious and eager to learn all available information; school groups may have specific learning objectives; senior citizens may attend simply to have an enjoyable time or learn something—adults over forty years old have often acquired a renewed interest in pursuing new areas of knowledge. Mental health organizations may use visits to museums as motivating or socializing experiences. Handicapped organizations may plan diverse programs for their members who may find it impossible to visit museums alone.

Every group thus has particular characteristics; understanding the profiles of different groups can help to plan tours. We will discuss school groups by age, gifted students, adults, families, minorities, handicapped, and visitors from other countries. We will review tour formats that work best for each group, and we will list unique characteristics or special suggestions where they may be applicable. **The information that can be shared with visitors depends on the general capabilities, motivations, and expectations of the persons who make up the tour group.**

SCHOOL AGE GROUPS

Children in school tour groups are prominent among museum audiences today. In past years, museum visits by children were not always seen as appropriate. In 1918, Benjamin Ives Gilman, the noted Secretary of the Boston Museum of Fine Arts, questioned whether children should be given any tours of the Boston museum. Works of art, he said, "were not made by children, nor, unless by exception, for children; and no aid can enable children to comprehend them fully" (Gilman, 1918, p. 285). Today, hopefully, docents discuss concepts in comprehensible terms and set tour goals that are within the grasp of all the young people in the group. And this means that current museum education methods are making tours more rewarding and pleasurable for school groups.

School groups often come on excursions, which teachers usually perceive to be complementary to class activities. Teachers have been accused of using field trips as entertainment or as a way of getting children out of the classroom. Indeed, they do not always think of the museum in educational terms. However, recent cooperative efforts between museums and schools have made visits of school children far more effective than in the past. More and more teachers attempt to prepare students for field trips and to make them relevant to class subjects. Unfortunately, there is a tendency among teachers to want students to see all of the exhibits, which may dilute the purpose of the trip and thus contribute minimally to classroom learning. School visits will never be effective, nor will they promote future museum visiting habits, if exposure is the main reason for the trips. It means very little simply to be in the presence of historical, artistic, or living objects. Tours can be effective, however, when museums are visited for specific purposes. The educator or interpreter should provide the basic subject matter and, after consultation with the teacher, present a tour that relates to current class subjects. The task becomes more difficult when teachers do not have specific reasons for coming. When this happens, the tour guide might ask what "units" or topics have been studied in recent weeks, and proceed from there.

Most school field trips are for students of elementary age. The classroom schedule is more flexible for lower than for upper grades because elementary school teachers are generalists. They remain with one or two classes throughout the day, and they can allow subjects to overlap. Schedules of high school students, on the other hand, are rigidly divided into time periods, with a different teacher for each subject. This not only segments learning, but also imposes a 50 to 60 minute class period during which the teacher must accomplish specific objectives. Students are involved in after-school jobs, sports activities, and a burgeoning social life. Field trips, therefore, become very difficult to schedule. If docents are scheduled to conduct a high school tour, they should consider it a singularly unusual opportunity.

Docents in art museums are particularly challenged to make school visits worthwhile. Among museums, art museums are visited least often by schools. As is generally known, visual arts are not considered "basic" by most school districts. With the exception of arts specialists, most teachers have little or no training in art, and they feel unable to use it in their teaching.

All museums are able to focus attention on actual objects, and thereby, they can provide unique educational experiences that schools cannot match. An opportunity to study original objects in concept-focused exhibits and to relate them to cultural, historical, or aesthetic information will be a new experience for most high school students. The challenge of deriving cultural meaning from objects is different from technical and scientific training, say, in the study of computer programming or biology. Most students are unfamiliar with strategies for using objects for study, particularly unusual or rare ones. Interpreters, therefore, must make every effort to design tours to complement the curriculum and to make the museum an important resource for the school. If this is not done, the educational potential of trips may be unrealized.

EARLY CHILDHOOD, ages 3 to 5

This age group accepts the world the way it seems to be; young children are not discriminating. Children may pick out an object that is different from all the rest, whether it is large or small. However, young children are unable to isolate appropriate information and disregard the rest. They are able to recognize common shapes such as squares, triangles, and circles, but at ages three to five, they are unable to classify anything logically or to categorize objects. While this group is curious about its world, it is highly egocentric. Young children are in the process of discovering themselves as individuals. A sense of other members of the community is growing. The total museum visit, therefore, from the moment they leave school to their return, can be important to children. The ride to the field trip site and the new surroundings can get the children so excited that they may have trouble concentrating on the tour. Children of this age are very verbal and may make many inappropriate comments, which are the product of their egocentric perceptions. Young children thus lack the necessary concepts for understanding their experiences. They lack the knowledge that would help them comprehend typical exhibits.

EFFECTIVE TOUR TECHNIQUES

Guided Discovery
Guided Involvement
Inquiry-Discussion

When using the Guided Discovery tour for this age group a more structured tour should be planned than for older children. This method can be interesting on a very simple level, but the structure must be very tight. Children cannot carry out a planned search because they are less able to discriminate and may not be able to find appropriate cues. The Inquiry-Discussion strategy, particularly when using comparisons of things **alike** and things **different,** is a good basis for questions and interaction with this group. Stories are important, whether based on fact or fiction. Sensory questions relating to tasting, touching, hearing, smelling and seeing are also helpful. Involving children in activities, particularly in historic sites that depict life in another era, can be exciting and intriguing to children of this age.

Suggestions and Guidelines

1. Discrimination can be improved by repetition and learning what is distinctive about an object.
2. In order to focus young children's attention, they should be actively involved in the tour.
3. All tours should contain some quiet activity; for example, while the children are seated in small groups.
4. Children of this age do not seem to understand that most art is the result of talent, training, and hard work. They are likely to believe that anyone can create art.

YOUNG CHILDREN, ages 6 to 7

This group is moving from an egocentric, "I am the center of the world," outlook toward a view of the world as it functions beyond their direct experience. They are acquiring a strong interest in their families, neighborhood, and school—they are beginning to participate socially in their world. Judgement and reasoning may not be fully developed, but feelings about things are up-front and in evidence. A belief in animism—that all things are alive and have feelings—is common. Imagination is strong, and children at this age learn actively through their senses. Motor skills are becoming more refined, and there is real interest in learning to make things.

Children are now beginning to organize their experiences by sorting things into different classes. They are becoming aware of the existence of other people and cultures. They may not understand that some things have existed longer than their own lives, or that some things no longer exist. Dinosaurs, for example, seem highly believable to them.

EFFECTIVE TOUR TECHNIQUES

Guided Discovery
Inquiry-Discussion

It is most important to remember the significance of this age group's relatively strong identification with concrete reality. Docents must present discussions from different perspectives. Although the power of imagination at this age level is limited, stories and imaginative problems can be used effectively with it. Both the Guided Discovery and the Inquiry-Discussion methods are useful tour strategies. These methods can lead to well-planned tours, if they allow students time to look individually and to make their own connections. With the Guided Discovery, however, guides must have definite methods for bringing the group back into a discussion, as they may get "off track" easily.

Suggestions and Guidelines

1. This group responds to identification of objects, analyses of similarities and differences, and appropriate vocabulary.
2. Most children at this age have trouble differentiating between their own perspective and that of the guide, particularly while looking at three dimensional objects. Children at this age assume everyone is seeing an object, painting, or environment in exactly the same way that they are seeing it. The part of an object which is hidden from some members of a group, yet is being discussed by the docent, has no meaning for them. It may not even seem to them to exist. (For further discussion on this subject see Chapter Three.) And for this reason, especially, guides should focus on different perspectives.
3. It is possible young children hear sounds differently than adults and cannot discriminate as effectively as adults when in crowds or noisy places. As they grow older, the ability to hear very high pitched sounds diminishes. When in museum settings, therefore, children may be unable to block out unwanted sounds or hear whispers. Interpreters must enunciate clearly and make sure they are heard.
4. Children at this age enjoy role-playing, and they take great delight in situations that require their imaginations. Interpreters should be sensitive to creating original learning experiences.
5. Children at this age observe detail, and guides may take advantage of this attribute.
6. Photographs may appeal to their realism, and they may be used to good effect.
7. Children have short attention spans and need to shift frequently from one mode of activity to another. Guides should emphasize active participation.
8. Students at this age cannot focus easily on small objects. Guides

should refer to obscure details in objects or exhibits only after large areas and obvious contexts are discussed.

9. Students like to touch real objects or close facsimiles. Contact with "real" objects makes tours more interesting.
10. Children at this age have limited eye-hand coordination and motor skills; workshops and hands-on activities should be planned accordingly.

OLDER CHILDREN, ages 8 to 11

Piaget considers this group as able to perceive the world outside its own experiences. It has greater awareness of how things really go together. It has begun to understand cause and effect. It can adapt information, exchange ideas and criticisms, and coordinate perspectives to hypothetical viewpoints. Ten to eleven year-olds are just beginning to be aware of the judgement of their peers, but they are not yet caught up in the pressures peers put on one another to achieve status. They are eager to explore, discover, and learn new things. There is a high level of absorption of new information, especially as it relates to concepts and experiences that they have known. Imagination is active, and it is greatly influenced by film and television images. Students of this age often hold relatively conventional expectations, since, up to this point, facts have been presented as "the way things are." In the museum, they are interested in why and how things were made, how long it took to make them, and what they were used for.

EFFECTIVE TOUR TECHNIQUES

Inquiry-Discussion or Guided Discovery

The most appropriate mode of presentation is that of Inquiry-Discussion, a combination of talking and listening by both guide and group members. When using this method, this age group is more likely to respond to questions and to interact, imagine, and discuss probabilities with a guide. Questions initiated by tour guides will encourage discussion, and in turn, student questions help guides know how the tour is progressing and to know what information they should draw upon. Guided Discovery techniques, allowing groups to disperse in the exhibit area with specific tasks, also are especially useful.

It is helpful to introduce natural or cultural connections at a very basic level with most students of this age, as they may not have sufficient knowledge in the subject area for drawing assumptions. In any case, it never hurts to hear fundamental information from a new source, particularly while looking at the original objects! Guides should include discussion of similarities and differences among objects. This practice not only helps guides focus on details of the objects, but it also serves to remind the group of concepts about the object and to let them hear the vocabulary needed to describe it.

Suggestions and Guidelines

1. At this age children will have spent a few years in school, and therefore, they will have some understanding of classroom procedures. The guide can build on their understanding with tour content that relates to classroom subjects.
2. Children will ask questions frequently and may compete with one another to answer questions correctly. Guides should be prepared to weave questions and answers into their presentations.
3. Children are literal minded at this age. The more a work of art resembles reality, the better youngsters think it is. They feel confident in their own opinions. Guides should be sensitive to the orientations children bring to tours.
4. At about eight years, children begin to realize that other people may see things differently than they do; now, they can infer what that other perspective may be. They become aware that other people have different thoughts and feelings. Guides might encourage children at this age to broaden their perspectives.
5. Children begin to have a greater awareness of facts and reality.
6. They can think about their actions and judge their own behavior.
7. Their expectation of beauty generally conforms to the standards of television and magazines.
8. They will want to please the interpreter and their teacher.
9. Children are apt to be high-spirited. Guides may use their enthusiasm in pursuit of discovery objectives.

EARLY ADOLESCENCE, age 12 to 14

Early adolescents are acquiring the ability to deal with abstractions—to "distill" experiences. This capacity develops unevenly in the 12 to 14 age group. As many as 75% of this age group have not completed the transition from thinking concretely about the here-and-now present to thinking in abstract terms with symbols and logic (National Commission on Resources for Youth, 1981). Because of rapid physical changes, unevenness in developing maturity, and tendencies to question authority, this age group can be one of the most difficult to guide. However, awareness of its limitations and potential can also make this group one of the most challenging and enjoyable with which to interact. Most young adolescents enjoy an unparalleled sense of fun and laughter; they like participating in the discovery of new ideas and other people's ways of doing things.

Although school systems group children chronologically by grade, the practice is somewhat inappropriate for early adolescents, since they vary so much in physical maturity, intellectual development, and social

TABLE TWO
OVERVIEW OF AUDIENCE CHARACTERISTICS

GROUP	CHARACTERISTICS	FREQUENCY OF VISITS	TOUR RECOMMENDATION
School: Early Childhood, 3-5	Egocentric; curious; non-discriminatory	Infrequent	Guided Discovery
School: Young Children, 6-7	Awareness of world; imaginative; refined motor skills	Infrequent	Guided Discovery
School: Older Children, 8-11	Socialized; allow interaction; literal minded	Frequent	Inquiry-Discussion/Guided Discovery
School: Early Adolescence, 12-14	Emerging sense of self	Frequent	Inquiry-Discussion/Guided Discovery
School: Adolescents, 14-18	Abstract thought; like realism; Goals: to get through school, go to college or get job	Infrequent	Inquiry-Discussion
Gifted Students, 5-18	Increased capacity for knowledge; gifted in one area or several; curious; unidentifiable by interpreter unless labeled	Infrequent as group	Guided Discovery
Young Adults, 18-30	Independent; interests: building career, starting family	Infrequent	Inquiry-Discussion
Adults, 30-62	Motivated by life needs and curiosity; knowledge acquisition	Frequent	Lecture-Discussion
Senior Adults, 62-	Similar to adults, but may be some physical limitations	Infrequent, depending on site location and area of country	Lecture-Discussion
Family Groups	Weekend visitors; reason for visit may be social interaction	Frequent, depending upon museum type	Guided Discovery Inquiry-Discussion
Minorities	Varied	Infrequent as group	Choice/Inquiry-Discussion
Handicapped	Varied	Infrequent	Choice
Out-of-Town, Foreign	Unfamiliar with area; may have specific interests	Depending upon site location	Inquiry-Discussion/Lecture-Discussion

abilities. Guides should be aware that individuals in this age group may be very different from one another. Physical changes are affected by advancing sexual maturity. In most girls, menstruation begins and their bodies assume more womanly shapes; in boys, voices change pitch, sexual feelings increase, and later, their bodies grow rapidly. Early adolescents, as a consequence, have a heightened sense of self-awareness. They are extremely conscious of the judgements of their peers. While it is very important to be part of the group, and to be approved of, preadolescents also want to feel unique and special in their personal identity and talents. At this time they begin to be aware of their limitations and to question their capacity to handle the future. Young adolescents are looking for new ways of doing things: they are beginning to seek independence, but they are also apprehensive about the world. This new introspection brings with it the need to feel a part of life's processes.

EFFECTIVE TOUR TECHNIQUES

Guided Discovery or Inquiry-Discussion

Groups of younger adolescents usually require adult supervision because they are too immature to show sufficient self-control over an extended period of time. While they are eager to contribute to group discussions, the guidance of the interpreter is necessary to provide direction. The recommended touring method is Inquiry-Discussion, which promotes interaction between members of the class and the adult interpreter. Many classes will benefit from peer guides, providing they are given sufficient preparation. Questions peers use should be specific and focused. The Guided Discovery is a less attractive alternative only because of the possibility of students being distracted from the tour objectives, but, given the right circumstances and a strong tour plan, it would be preferred. A Guided Discovery tour should be one which "works" and has a real possibility of success. Another effective tour might involve combined aspects of each method.

Suggestions and Guidelines

1. Socializing is important in adolescence, and the freedom the museum provides from classroom restrictions creates an excellent opportunity for young people to talk about the new environment and discuss the exhibits among themselves. The Guided Discovery method offers a basis for structuring discussion, and it still allows sufficient flexibility. Without discipline and guidance, however, the tour could be chaos.
2. Young adolescents enjoy a sophisticated "adult" setting. They want to be treated like adults. Guides should be sure that the adolescents know the "rules" of the tour, so that they need not be

constantly corrected. If possible, they should be allowed to make some decisions.

3. Guides should ensure that the tour has meaning. The adolescents should know clearly what they have learned or accomplished when the tour is over. Guides should avoid jargon and big words.

ADOLESCENCE, ages 14 to 18

Young people aged 14 to 18 should be considered adults in their ability to think abstractly and to make connections between concepts. At this age, students can act upon more than one abstraction at a time and use rather sophisticated logic. They should have some background, however slight, in fundamental areas of the museum. They now have a basic understanding of differences in world cultures, and of the times in which cultural changes occurred.

Motivation for learning among adolescents, however, is not the same as for adults. Students in secondary school (and some college students) are often motivated to learn subject matter, in an organized, structured manner. Many students have not made connections between learning and life's experiences. Learning thus will begin to take on real meaning when these adolescents become adults. Open discussion may or may not have been much of a part of their educational experience.

Many of the problems associated with touring adolescents are similar to those for preadolescents. These young people can be egotistical, preoccupied with the opposite sex, self-conscious about how they look, and sensitive about how others are judging them. Many do not want to be singled out for attention, and therefore, they may seem disinterested and unresponsive.

Adolescents are highly susceptible to peer pressure, and they are fearful of "looking stupid." Therefore, they are the least likely of all age groups to respond to questions. The idea of divergent questions—those that stimulate many possible answers—is not likely to appeal to them, unless a situation of complete trust is established. They are inclined to reject what they do not want to see, feel, or learn about. In general, they cannot be expected to react maturely to museum objects.

Adolescents do understand, nonetheless, that people can make a contribution to society. They recognize that objects, particularly artistic ones, embrace differences of opinion and attitudes and that values held about them are open to interpretation. As with younger adolescents, they prefer traditional, realistic objects. Whether the object is unique does not matter. Although historic objects may seem to have more value because of their antiquity, antique items generally do not interest adolescents. According to Gardner, issues of artistic integrity are not of concern to teenagers because they do not have the occasion to deal with such issues (Gardner, 1982).

High school students make up "only 10% or less of all student visitors to museums" (O'Connell, 1981, p. 2). Generally, high school students feel ill at ease in a museum, and its collections and exhibits seem not to relate to their lives. Visits to zoos and historical areas, on the other hand, are less structured; therefore, they are more relaxed, understandable environments. Only a few museums offer programs that appeal specifically to teenagers. The Indianapolis Museum, for example, has appealed to adolescents through "Search" programs which have attempted to demonstrate that museum objects can be "read" in different ways and can provide insights into their lives. The Brooklyn Museum appealed to teens through their "collector's instinct;" the museum reasoned that all young people collect objects and could be attracted to the museum by tapping into that interest. It found that most students in the Brooklyn area had used museums in pursuit of school subjects, yet they were unaware of ways to analyze or speculate about exhibits in any other context. Apparently, this was because the most important issues in the lives of adolescents who use museums are school work and economic livelihood. In other words, these youth want to get through school, go to college or get a good job, and make money. School for them was more a means to an end than a source of contemplation (Andrews, 1981).

EFFECTIVE TOUR TECHNIQUES

Inquiry-Discussion
Guided Discovery

The type of tour that is appropriate gradually moves from participatory to more structured learning as the age of the school group increases. The emphasis now is on involving young people in the tour. Tours will be best if groups are no larger than about five to eight students.

The most effective method is the Inquiry-Discussion Method, but only if the groups are kept small. A modified lecture tour can be appropriate, particularly when used as a tour introduction, but it can quickly become tedious if it is lengthened. Guides should avoid becoming an extension of the classroom by too much lecturing. The quality of the discussion will depend upon the profile of the group, the familiarity of members with each other, and the learning climate fostered in their classroom at school. If their teacher has encouraged discussion, there will be fewer inhibiting fears. Guides should present open-ended questions relating to interpretation, meaning, and values, and encourage generalizations. After consultation and planning with the teacher, guides might use the Guided Discovery tour effectively, especially when students are given problem-solving tasks which encourage involvement in the material being presented.

It is important in motivating adolescent learning to associate information being presented with personal and school experiences. Teachers usually want exhibits that emphasize school subject-matter or concepts that are general enough for them to relate to classroom topics.

We must remember that guides who work often with this trend-setting age group should be acquainted with the current interests of adolescents. Guides may lose credibility when they hold ideas about adolescents that are out-of-date.

Suggestions and Guidelines

1. Interpreters must be sincere and show an interest in each adolescent as an individual. Negative attitudes are communicated easily to adolescents who may become on guard during a tour.
2. Because student attitudes and behaviors may change quickly, docents should be prepared to change also, from being cooperative to being authoritative, interested, etc.
3. Interpreters should acknowledge and recognize whatever adolescents may be feeling about the exhibit and the museum.
4. High school students usually will not "play games;" if they are talked down to, they may be "turned off" for the entire tour. Indeed, they may arrive with a poor attitude, since they may think of field trips as appropriate mainly for elementary schools.
5. Adolescents prefer not to speculate or guess—they do not want to look ridiculous or be wrong. Therefore guides may find it difficult to draw answers to questions from them.
6. Students at this age are able to work cooperatively with other members of a group. This allows opportunity for creative tour planning and for implementing the Discovery or Inquiry strategy.
7. Many youths will test the authority of tour guides to control them. Guides may overcome this by adopting a mutual problem-solving strategy, which may motivate the adolescents to think of new and unusual ideas rather than power relationships.
8. Adolescents may not expect museums to contribute anything to their lives. A highly relevant tour can be inspiring.

MIXED AGE GROUPS

THE GIFTED STUDENT

Attitudes toward the gifted have fluctuated over the past hundred years. Long ago, geniuses were thought to be so abnormal that they were perceived as evil. Today, society accepts the gifted child; however, because these young people are so able, bright, and talented, they are expected to be motivated to realize their potential on their own. Discussions abound among educators concerning the best way to nurture the talent of the gifted. Two major methods of educating the gifted, however, have evolved. They are usually called the "enrichment" and "acceleration" methods, respectively. In simplified form, the enrichment method provides numerous intellectual and cultural opportunities for young people. Through various means, it trains their minds in problem-solving and creativity. The accelerated method of learning advances young people in subjects in which they are found to be superior. It allows them to progress at their own rates into areas of increasing complexity. Each approach has its vigorous proponents, and for our purposes, it is not important to discuss which method is better. However, students are usually identified by tests for admission to either type of program. For example, on IQ tests, school districts may select those whose scores exceed a minimum score of 130 for eligibility to their gifted programs. Some schools also attempt to identify and encourage students who are talented in the arts. These young people are selected for a gifted program most often via teacher nominations. There are a number of "magnet" schools throughout the country which segregate and train young people who are talented in art, music, dance, or theatre in addition to their regular basic subjects.

The intellectually gifted are the students that most tour guides will encounter in their classes, workshops, and tours. Because of the prevalence of the enrichment method, field trips will most likely have been planned from the perspective of teachers as enrichment activities. They intend them to add to students' knowledge and to expose them to different aspects of "culture." It is important, therefore, to relate the tour information to subjects that are being studied in school.

EFFECTIVE TOUR TECHNIQUES

Guided Discovery
Inquiry-Discussion
Guided Involvement

Groups of gifted individuals should be allowed flexibility during the tour and time to pursue special projects or areas of interest. The Guided Discovery format is highly appropriate for the gifted. A great deal of learning is in the search. Ideally, teachers should be consulted ahead of time so that interpreters can know which subjects are being studied at the time a tour is scheduled. Problem-solving through studying objects and exhibits is an ideal strategy, particularly if interpreters can follow up and reinforce ideas. Small group discussion will be more educational than the lecture method. Above all, docents must challenge gifted students to reach beyond their classroom assignments to find creative connections and hypothetical solutions to problems. Gifted students share an unusual capacity for dealing with facts and knowledge and a voracious curiosity. These students may know about more areas than one might expect of persons their age because of the extensive reading that they do.

The Inquiry-Discussion is a less satisfactory, but suitable method. The emphasis, when using this technique, would be on discussion, which should not dominate the tour but evolve from the objects and exhibits.

The Guided Involvement technique, at a higher level of abstraction than merely going through the motions, is also adequate. Cooking, blacksmithing, or painting cannot satisfy true curiosity without a tie-in to the human condition through history, politics, labor, etc. For example, when discussing such topics with the gifted, guides should talk about the economic or technological limitations of colonial life, the reasons for changing painting styles, or the variety of ways reality has been interpreted in the arts.

Suggestions and Guidelines

1. The gifted are similar physically to other children. They are not smaller in stature, they are not unhealthy, nor do they "burn out" when they are adults. Intellectually gifted children as a group are as socially and emotionally mature as other students.
2. Educational acceleration is not harmful, as some believe.
3. Gifted girls tend to be perceived by their classmates more negatively than gifted boys.
4. Many people hold negative stereotypes of the gifted, thinking of them as odd (Stanley, 1980).

YOUNG ADULTS, ages 18 to 30

The structured group settings of formalized schooling are, for the most part, over for young adults. They are now specializing in areas of further study or the workplace, and they are beginning to concentrate on mastering particular subjects and activities. They are scattered from their families, and they are involved in their personal lives. Their interests generally do not include visiting museums. Such priorities as pursuing a job, attending a college or university, or earning a living, preoccupy them. In short, building careers and starting families are the most important concerns to this age group. Leisure time is usually spent in sports activities, socializing with friends, or other forms of entertainment. Museum visits become important pastimes to young adults as leisure activities when their families are involved or when a rare, highly publicized object or collection is to be viewed.The casual gathering of information in museums is not part of the lives of most young adults.

EFFECTIVE TOUR TECHNIQUES

Inquiry-Discussion
Lecture-Discussion
Guided Discovery

When groups of this general age level book a museum tour, it is likely that they have a specific reason for coming. Docents should determine the purpose of the visit so that the tour may be planned and focused.

Inquiry-Discussion is the most effective technique because it promotes interaction. Whether a Lecture-Discussion tour would be useful depends on the interests of the group. They may want to acquire as much information as they can about a particular subject. Guided Discovery can be an effective option when the guide believes that the young people would get more out of the exhibit with a short opening lecture and a self-guided tour. This approach would allow them to follow their own interests and timetable. It is important that they are provided with sufficient information, perhaps in a handout, about the exhibit.

THE ADULT VISITOR

Adults have a rich store of life experiences. They have undergone a formal system of education, which established teachers as authority figures and learners as having either right or wrong answers. For some, schooling will have produced interest in continued learning; for others, it may have produced scars. Most adults understand, however, that there are many sources of knowledge other than that in formal classrooms. Personal goals and curiosity now motivate the adult, and a great deal of both informal and formal learning will occur throughout adulthood (Knowles, 1981, p. 54). When adults do return to the setting of formal schooling, they are usually trying to address a particular task in life—a new job, a move to a new city, or retirement. Competition for an adult's recreational time thus can be intense.

Adults learn in different ways than children. **Fluid intelligence**—discovering ideas and relations through reasoning—involves "short-term memory" and grows rapidly during childhood and usually reaches its peak in adolescence. If these reasoning processes are not practiced, they may decline during the adult years. **Crystallized intelligence**—using and building on knowledge stored in long-term memory is dependent on education and experience. Knowledge should accumulate in adulthood; thus, crystallized intelligence should increase with age (Knowles, 1981, p. 55).

Most adults on tours have deliberately sought out the experience. People come to museums (and interpreters undergo training classes) to increase their knowledge in an enjoyable context. They want to feel good about themselves (build self-esteem) and acquire a fulfilling experience during their leisure time. Adults come to particular exhibits after they have read about them. They may be eager to find out about the history of an area or the background of an object, that is, how it was made or used. They may have little use for the specific information, but it may provide insight into something familiar but poorly understood. For example: Are the King Tut treasures similar to the gold objects we prize today? Were they fashioned in a similar manner? What do the original paintings of the Impressionists look like? How do painters see reality? What kind of farm or kitchen implements did our great-grandparents use when they settled in the West?

EFFECTIVE TOUR TECHNIQUES

Lecture-Discussion
Inquiry-Discussion

The Lecture-Discussion mode of presentation is highly satisfactory for adult visitors, especially when a great deal of interaction occurs. Guides should consider the motivation or reason for the group's visit. Random groups on a Sunday afternoon may or may not be responsive to a discussion format, while preorganized groups with some background or interest in the subject may carry on lively discussions with guides. Since adults do a great deal of learning on their own, they often enjoy partly self-directed tours, in which they establish their own pathways to learning.

Docents should avoid alienating adult visitors by conducting tours as though they were formal classes. If lectures are so highly structured that adults feel that they are being treated as "students," they may experience the whole museum visit in a negative way. Adults are responsible for their own lives, and they will probably choose to ignore a guide who talks down to them. "If museum professionals start teaching adults as if they were children, pretty soon adults are going to feel that museums are just like schools" (Knowles, 1981, p. 59). It is important, therefore, that mode of delivery and information be appropriate to adult needs and interests. Even when adults have little or no background in a particular subject, they can often find something in their own experiences that will connect with the information being offered.

The museum/historical site is particularly well suited for relating information uniquely to environmental, technological, and cultural life—past and present. If exhibits are interpreted on the basis of their relevance to past, present, or future cultural contexts, adults may be motivated strongly to participate in the discussion.

SENIOR ADULTS

By 1990 the over-65 age group will constitute more than 50% of the national population.Senior adults have as many different learning capabilities, backgrounds, and experiences as any other adult age group. They may come to a museum as preorganized groups based on where they live (apartment complexes, retirement homes, etc.), other organizations to which they belong (AARP, church groups, community recreation centers), or they may come together for specific learning purposes (Elder Hostels, continuing education programs, community classes). Tour guides sometimes underestimate the elderly. They tend to think of them as preferring bland material or lacking interest in the museum exhibits.

In the years ahead, we can expect people to reach older adulthood with more formal educational backgrounds, higher income levels, and increased social influence. Retirement ages are lower today than ever before, and older adults have more leisure time. Older adults are also more physically fit than ever, and they lead active lives. Only five percent of all elderly are institutionalized.

EFFECTIVE TOUR TECHNIQUES

Lecture-Discussion
Inquiry-Discussion

Both Lecture-Discussion and Inquiry-Discussion methods are excellent for older adults. Both draw upon give and take, and they involve adults in ways which enable them to contribute information from their own life experiences. Tour guides thus can take advantage of the wisdom and rich life experiences that older adults bring to museums.

Museum guides should remember that physical limitations may accompany advancing years whereas mental powers for learning may remain sharp. Senior citizens in tour groups will have diverse capacities for hearing and vision. Further, differences in their stamina for walking and standing will be considerable. There is no way for docents to prepare for all eventualities; therefore, guides must be sensitive to cues from the group itself. The suggestions in the Adult section of this chapter hold true for the senior adult. Although some adults may leave a tour group—to proceed at their own pace—many will want to learn all they can from knowledgeable guides.

Suggestions and Guidelines

1. The vision of older adults adapts more slowly from light to dark; they need to move gradually from well-lit areas to dark areas and from outdoors into dim corridors.
2. A loss of visual sharpness occurs in older people, and they need increased illumination for clear vision.
3. Color perceptions may change; blues and greens are less distinct than reds and oranges.
4. Background noises may interfere with hearing. Guides should speak in quiet corners or secluded areas. They should speak as loudly as possible.
5. Tour guides should avoid asking older adults to stand or walk for long periods.
6. Glare may be a problem; tour guides should not stand or place objects in front of brightly lit cases.
7. The visual field narrows and peripheral vision lessens.
8. Depth perception weakens; guides should take special care on stairways.

TABLE THREE
RECOMMENDED TOUR TECHNIQUES

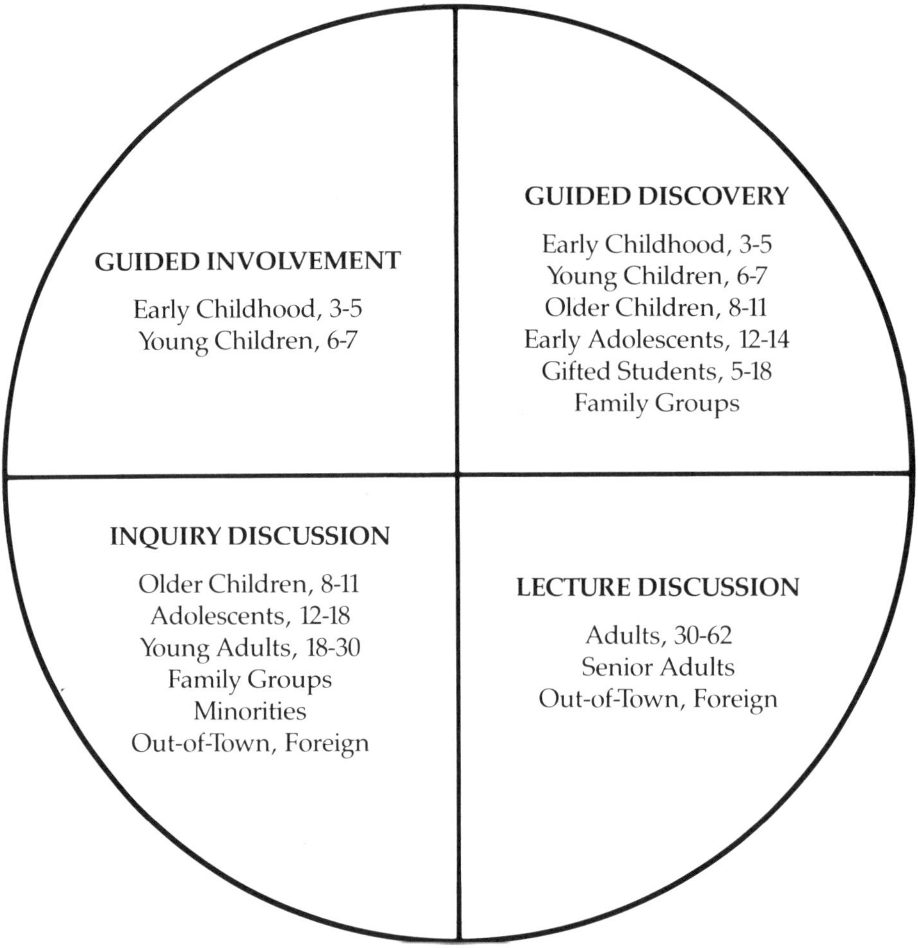

GUIDED INVOLVEMENT

Early Childhood, 3-5
Young Children, 6-7

GUIDED DISCOVERY

Early Childhood, 3-5
Young Children, 6-7
Older Children, 8-11
Early Adolescents, 12-14
Gifted Students, 5-18
Family Groups

INQUIRY DISCUSSION

Older Children, 8-11
Adolescents, 12-18
Young Adults, 18-30
Family Groups
Minorities
Out-of-Town, Foreign

LECTURE DISCUSSION

Adults, 30-62
Senior Adults
Out-of-Town, Foreign

THE FAMILY GROUP

No group is as perplexing to analyze before a tour as the family. Its characteristics are difficult to categorize, and preparing for it is hard. In reality, we are dealing with the widest range of possibilities and motives, for in visiting a museum, "family members freely choose to come to the museum; they need no prerequisites or credentials; they are heterogeneous learner groups with respect to age, background, and interests and attach great importance to social interaction as an ingredient of their visit" (Laetsch, 1980, p. 2). The time spent at the museum is considered recreational; learning is a by-product. Family members are together to be with one another and to discuss what they see in the exhibits. When children are young, parents may take them about the museum, showing them exhibits that they think will be especially interesting to them. Excursions to zoos, for example, are popular for several reasons: the zoo environment is not intimidating; children are unrestrained physically; they can become excited and reasonably noisy; parents rarely have to discipline them; and picnic facilities are often available. An educational experience is thus often one of the least important reasons for visiting a zoo.

Consider a study conducted at the Berkeley Lawrence Hall of Science. Family groups spent an average of two hours at the museum. They moved quickly from exhibit to exhibit. "Only 18% of the exhibits received the attention of visitors for more than three minutes" (Laetsch, 1982, p. 12). Family discussions dealt more with concrete than with abstract impressions.

Most families visit museums on weekends, and unless a special activity is scheduled, they may wish to pursue their own interests independently. When in the museum or historical area, however, parents may become sufficiently familiar with the museum's surroundings or collections to make the next trip even more fulfilling for themselves and their family.

EFFECTIVE TOUR TECHNIQUES

Guided Discovery
Inquiry-Discussion
Lecture-Discussion

The best tour for the family is the Guided Discovery, since it is interesting to persons of all ages. But because tours for family groups cannot be planned accurately, tour guides should be prepared to move to an Inquiry-Discussion format.

It is difficult to focus tours for family members simultaneously. When a tour involves several families, the tour technique may have to be compromised because members of the group will have such different relationships with one another. Some will be intimately related and others will be strangers. Certainly there will be members of different generations. Adults in the group, however, are likely to be anxious to assist the youngsters in their families, so messages of tour guides can generally be directed at the level of the children. Interpreters in National Parks will find most of their audiences are families who are vacationing or on day-long outings. Guides should involve such groups through inquiry, encourage them to ask questions, and probe for their interests.

Workshops present opportunity for focused family activities. Parents may become helpers and spend workshop time assisting their children. Workshops can give children opportunities to create and construct their own work without parental assistance, too.

Suggestions and Guidelines

1. The family will want to stay together except for short problem-solving activities. Tours should encourage their togetherness.
2. One of the most important reasons for a family experience, from the viewpoint of the parents, is to do something for and with their children. The adults will be satisfied when the children are busy and interested.
3. All members of the family can be reached by involving the adults in either the Inquiry-Discussion or the Guided Discovery technique.
4. Difficult family relationships are best ignored, even though the museum experience may be diminished. Family interaction is a private matter.

MINORITIES

Almost all nations of the world are represented in the United States. The predominant ethnic minorities are Blacks, Hispanics, Chinese, and Japanese; each has contributed its rich heritage to our contemporary culture. There are also hundreds of thousands of others from countless countries. All of these people possess customs, cherished religious artifacts, and contemporary and historic art objects. In every ethnic group and culture, certain things will be prized for their beauty and rarity. However, it has not been in the tradition of all cultures to maintain and preserve exceptional artistic or historic collections for public display or study, or to document cultural heritage.

Minorities—Blacks, Hispanics, and other ethnic groups—are the new audiences for museums. In past years, these groups attempted to assimilate themselves silently and invisibly into the predominately Western culture. But many cultural traditions were maintained in either ethnic organizations or in families. Recently, pride in group heritage has surfaced. Everyone may now benefit from new opportunities to learn about different philosophies and experience new traditions. It is enriching for all to acknowledge diversity in beauty and artistic accomplishment. Minorities thus exert a strong and growing impact on the life and culture of the United States. They are having considerable influence on museums as both policy makers and audiences.

Minorities have not traditionally come to museums in large numbers. One of the primary reasons for low attendance is that most exhibits and public programs reflect a bias toward Western civilization. Museums, with few exceptions, have made little effort to reach out. The opening in recent years of Afro-American, Native American, and other folk art museums in all parts of the country has heightened museum interest in cultural diversity.

Contemporary tour guides, therefore, must be sensitive to the cultural plurality of audiences today. Tour guides should assume responsibility for learning about the traditions and treasures of local minority groups. Native Americans of the Southwest, for example, have preserved many ancient beliefs and practices. The Native American child is living between two worlds—one represents the American culture of today, and the other, one that thrived before the Caucasians and other ethnicities came to America. It is common for tribe members to speak two languages, live in the ancestral manner in hogans or pueblos, eat traditional foods, and yet, share in the wider society. Within Native American cultures, as in many ethnic groups, members many be divided by their value orientations in three ways: (1) the traditionalists who keep to the old religious and cultural patterns, (2) the moderates who believe in their heritage, but have adjusted to the dominant culture. (3) the progressives who wish to abandon the old cultural patterns and adopt modern values and beliefs (Roessel, 1975).

Native Americans are not unique among ethnic groups in living in each of two cultures. All ethnic groups are absorbed into the dominant culture to a greater or lesser degree; traditionalists in all cultures treasure the beautiful and try to keep unique customs alive. Since an appropriate learning environment begins with a relaxed, receptive group, tour guides who are sensitive to the breadth of cultural values in our society are in the best position to help audiences from minority ethnic groups appreciate the complementary aspects of cultural differences.

EFFECTIVE TOUR TECHNIQUES

Inquiry-Discussion
Lecture-Discussion
Guided Discovery (young people)

Through prestudy or inquiry the docent should learn whether a particular feature of an exhibit may be of special interest to members of a given ethnic group. In general, ethnicity is not a factor in determining which tour technique to use. The Inquiry-Discussion technique has the advantage, however, of providing the docent with an opportunity to glean insights from the group which might strengthen tour discussion. Only when the guide is aware of language problems need there be conscious modification of the tour plan.

THE HANDICAPPED

Our culture has been insensitive to the needs and capabilities of the handicapped. Handicapped people, for example, have been denied access to museums and other historical institutions largely because of architectural obstructions. A person is handicapped who "has a physical or mental impairment which substantially limits one or more major life activities—functions such as caring for one's self, performing manual tasks, walking, seeing, hearing, speaking, breathing, learning, and working" (Federal Regulation 504). Federal regulations, enacted in 1973, require that new buildings provide ease of access for handicapped persons; they require, too, that modifications be made in older structures in order to open them to the handicapped. Consequently, programs are now designed to allow the handicapped full participation in the cultural and educational life of the community. Accessibility means more than just accommodating people in terms of mobility; it means also accessibility to information and to guided tours regarding exhibits. Interpreters must be able to tour people with all kinds of disabilities and handicaps.

EFFECTIVE TOUR TECHNIQUES

Interpreters should tailor the tour technique to the nature of the disability. The Lecture-Discussion method in general may be least appropriate. We recommend involving during the tour more than one sensory experience, if possible. When the blind can touch and the deaf can make visual interpretations, for example, the tour has a better chance of success. Interpreters should consult with the agency, school, or other sources of origin for the tour to determine the objectives for it. Since tour guides are not expected to be experts in dealing with various handicapping conditions, the tour originator must also provide an adequate number of assistants to accompany the group. That is, tour guides should be able to rely on the sponsoring organization to help determine the appropriateness of subject matter, proper tour length, and extent of support required from assisting adults.

There are differences between handicapped and disabled persons. "A **disability** is a decrease in the functioning of a part, or perhaps a system, of the human body. A **handicap** is a disability that interferes with normal activities which would include involvements with media, movement, and performance" (Barlow, 1978, p. 56). Let us now consider the following important forms of disability:

SPEECH AND LANGUAGE IMPAIRMENT

This disability can be the result of hearing loss, cerebral palsy, cleft palate, mental retardation, or emotional disturbance. Speech impairments can be stuttering, voice disorders (loudness, pitch, or quality), or articulation. They are usually not temporary. Many persons have no other handicaps. Even though they may have articulation problems, for example, they are likely to possess intellectual skills comparable to other persons. Language impairment can be due to difficulty in understanding other people or problems with speaking.

HEARING IMPAIRMENT

Deafness is now more common in very young children than in older children, because modern medicines have reduced illnesses leading to deafness in early childhood. When a hearing problem arises in children it is often accompanied by speech impairment, because hearing distorted sounds at diminished volume makes it difficult for them to reproduce the correct sounds.

Adults lose their hearing with advancing age, illness, or injury. They are better able to understand sounds than those who have been deaf since infancy, because they were hearing persons during their formative years. Deafness in the elderly usually signifies being hard-of-hearing, which means that the elderly often can make some sense out of the sounds around them.

The **deaf** are thought of as those persons who cannot function with or without a hearing aid. Those who are **hard-of-hearing** have impaired hearing, but hearing aids may restore listening capabilities to them.

Suggestions and Guidelines

1. Tour guides should face the hearing impaired person. They will watch the guide, or read lips, and, then, turn to look at what is being discussed. Of course, their turning away does not indicate that they have lost interest.
2. If an interpreter for the deaf (sign language) is available, signing should be done to one side, in view of all the group.
3. Tour guides should keep their hands away from their mouths when speaking.
4. Tour guides should speak slowly.
5. Tour guides may have to repeat comments. All questions should be repeated for the whole group.
6. Tour guides should avoid standing in front of windows, (the back lighting may prevent the guides' face from being seen clearly) or moving about the room.

VISUAL DISABILITIES

The major causes of blindness are diabetes, cataracts, glaucoma, and accidents. About one-third of the blind population can read some braille (National Arts and the Handicapped Information Service, 1978). Blind persons are able to function extremely well, and they should not be directed to exhibits for the blind only. Tour guides should adopt meaningful descriptive terms that will depict exhibits accurately.

Finding exhibits that can be understood in other than visual terms is the main problem of the blind. It is important to provide braille labels, touchable exhibits, and descriptive cassette tours. The visually disabled should be as comfortable as the sighted in a museum.

The visually disabled range from people whose vision has been corrected with glasses to those who are legally blind and who "see" by touch and hearing. Tours should emphasize those exhibits that are very well lit and can be reached by simple routes. Exhibits must be chosen carefully, for people who cannot see well are unable to pick out details.

The National Arts and the Handicapped Information Service (1978) provides the following suggestions for tour guides:

1. Provide one volunteer for about every five people, which allows guides to give individual attention.
2. Tell the blind person to use both hands when touching an artifact, which helps them gain a better understanding of it.
3. Blind children are different from blind adults. They are often more sophisticated in their adaption to blindness; their approach to art will be more like that of a sighted person.
4. Tour guides should avoid sudden surprises, watch for things that move unexpectedly, and keep from making noises.

LEARNING DISABILITIES

Learning disabled people suffer disorders, associated with comprehension and conceptualization, that affect the ways they understand and use spoken or written language. Their problems usually are not due to mental retardation or emotional disturbances. They may be distractable, hyperactive, and socially immature. Guides should be aware that the learning disabled child or adolescent may compulsively explore the museum and might be destructive at times. Groups with learning disabled members usually will be accompanied by a sufficient number of special teachers or adults who can deal with unusual behaviors.

MENTAL RETARDATION

Mentally retarded individuals do not learn as fast as other people. Their brains, which may have been damaged genetically or in accidents, work slowly. Thus, it often takes longer for the retarded to learn social rules as well as school subjects. Tour guides should look to accompanying teachers for guidance, and they should follow their advice accordingly.

OUT-OF-TOWN OR FOREIGN VISITORS

Many people who come to museums or historic sites are there to view a specific collection or exhibit, or simply to spend leisure time. Their interests range from passive interest to genuine curiosity. They may be determined to "see-it-all." If several drop-in visitors end up on the same tour, the docent will have a diversified group of many ages and interests. The tour guide thus should question members of the group to learn of specific interests that might be developed for discussion.

SOME CULTURAL DIFFERENCES IN BODY-LANGUAGE

England: Handshakes are acceptable, in a friendly, but somewhat reserved manner. Guides should be punctual and begin the tour at the assigned time. Of course, English is the official language, but there are many dialects; tour guides may find some words are difficult to understand.

Australia: People like to be called by their first names and greeted with a handshake. Tour guides should not shake hands with a woman unless she offers her hand first. Eye contact should be maintained with those in the group. A clenched fist with raised thumb (similar to hitchhiking) is a vulgar gesture. English is the official language.

China: A nod or bow is a sign of courtesy when greeting someone. The Chinese are formal with introductions, and they do not like to be touched by strangers. They have very good manners, and they are hospitable.

France: Shaking hands is the way people are greeted. A man should not offer his hand to a woman first. It is courteous to be punctual.

Germany: Germans are relatively reserved and restrained. Northern Germans may be very formal. It is considered disrespectful to talk with one's hands in one's pockets.

India: Some Indians do not shake hands or touch women in either formal or informal gatherings, but educated women will shake hands with Westerners. Modesty and humility are important values to many women.

Japan: The traditional greeting is a bow; however, handshakes are being used more and more.

Mexico: The usual greeting is a nod or handshake. Mexican people typically stand close to one another while talking. They are generally very friendly and polite.

Organized groups make up a large part of audiences who visit museums. Both within each group and across different groups, purposes for visiting museums and interest in exhibits may vary greatly. Touring techniques may need to be adjusted to fit the circumstances. When we classify visitors on the bases of the characteristics that bring people together in a museum, tour guides may obtain clues as to why the individuals have come to the museum, and importantly, they may obtain indication as to ways in which the tour can be planned to make it more interesting and enjoyable. The following chart summarizes briefly the group characteristics discussed in this chapter, the frequency with which such groups are likely to visit a museum or historical site, and the touring techniques recommended throughout the chapter for the groups.

REFERENCES

American Council for the Arts. (1981). **Americans and the Arts.** (Research conducted by the National Center of the Arts, Inc.). New York: author.

Andrews, K. (1981). Raising a low profile: urban teens and urban museums. **Roundtable Reports: The Journal of Museum Education, 6**(4), 6-9.

Barlow, G. C. (1978). The nature of society's attitude toward the handicapped and the arts. **The Arts and Handicapped People: Defining the National Direction.** Washington DC: The National Committee, Arts for the Handicapped. 56-60.

Gardner, H. (1982). **Art, Mind and Brain.** New York: Basic Books.

Gilman, B. I. (1918). **Museum Ideals of Purpose and Method.** Cambridge, Massachusetts: Riverside Press.

Knowles, M. S. (1981). Andragogy. In Z. W. Collins (Ed.) **Museums, Adults and the Humanities, A Guide for Educational Programming.** Washington, DC: American Association of Museums.

Laetsch, W. M. (1980). **Science and Children,** cited by I. Wolins, in **Roundtable Reports: The Journal of Museum Education, 7**(1), p. 2.

Laetsch, W. M. (1982). Taking a measure of families. **Roundtable Reports: The Journal of Museum Education, 7**(1), 3-13.

National Arts and the Handicapped Information Service. (1978). **Arts for Blind and Visually Impaired People.** Washington, DC: Author.

National Commission on Resources for Youth. (1981). **New Roles for Early Adolescents.** New York: Author.

National Research Center of the Arts. (1973). **Arts and the People, A Survey of Public Attitudes and Participation in the Arts and Culture in New York State.** 71-73. New York: American Council for the Arts in Education.

O'Connell, P. (1981). Teenagers in the museum: may the force be with you. **Roundtable Reports: The Journal of Museum Education, 64,** 2-9.

Roessel, R. A. (1975). **Handbook for Indian Education.** Tempe, Arizona: Arizona State University.

Stanley, J. C. (1980). On educating the gifted. **Educational Researcher.** March, 8-12.

CHAPTER SEVEN
The Personal Guide

Developing a Style • Audience Interaction • Verbal Communication • NonVerbal Communication: What We Don't Say

Art objects, historic objects and unique environments communicate to viewers even without an interpreter. The meaning of the experience, however, depends upon each viewer's prior experience and knowledge. When we, as tour guides or docents, communicate exhibit information, we must consider (1) the nature of the exhibit, (2) the familiarity of objects to visitors, (3) the ways information is presented to visitors and (4) the interpretations visitors make of the message. Tour guides and visitors must share an understanding of the "communication system" in order to exchange information efficiently and effectively with one another (Winner, 1984). In Chapter Seven we deal with how we communicate information, verbally and nonverbally, and how we can help visitors understand it correctly.

When we communicate, we must be sensitive to cues important in interpersonal interaction. How successfully we recognize and utilize these cues determines whether or not we convey our message. Each of us can cultivate a personal style of interaction by mastering verbal and nonverbal communication skills. Verbal communication can be garbled by word choice, bad organization, or poor delivery. Nonverbal communication "sends" subtle but powerful messages. While we speak, our facial and body gestures may emphasize or conflict with our spoken words. A well-modulated voice and relaxed posture will underscore a message. We should use audience reactions to evaluate ourselves and our tour effectiveness. We must be confident and sufficiently flexible to alter the tour plan wherever it seems appropriate. When verbal and nonverbal messages are coordinated and presented in understandable fashion, tour guides and visitors alike are able to use the same social benchmarks for communicating with one another.

The goal of Chapter Seven is to help interpreters become better "performers" via style and technique so that the information they offer during tours will become "real and meaningful" to visitors. "Style" may be defined as the manner in which our personality and behavior affect the tour. The way in which we communicate, how we appear to the visitor, and the "body language" we use influence the success of a tour. "Technique" is defined as the format, content, and other related activities associated with the presentation. There is no single definition of the perfect tour, but definitely there are methods that can improve the quality of a presentation. With practice, it is not difficult to combine "style" and "technique;" to be in control of both, is the hallmark of "the good guide."

DEVELOPING A STYLE

Should tour guides be concerned about how visitors regard them? It is not necessary to appear "learned" before groups, to be "the leader," or to impress other docents. Personal style, however, can be improved consciously through rehearsal of various techniques of communication, both visual and verbal. Style can be improved by watching performers in action, live or on television, or by noting the style of other successful tour guides. Sometimes it may be helpful for those who have "quiet" personalities to adopt some of the skills of the extrovert when touring; perhaps an expressive voice and more appropriate body language should be acquired, without being too unnatural. The essence of a successful interpretive "performance" stems from a sincere, personal style.

THE GUIDE AS A PERFORMING ARTIST

Guides, like good teachers and actors, interact with an audience. They present exhibit interpretations in a specific setting. At times, tour guides must feel they are on stage, performing for visitors. Since interpretation is an art, guides really are actors. The "performance" is intended to inspire, enthuse, and inform the audience about the subject. However, guides must not simply deliver a soliloquy and wait for applause. Effective communication with audiences involves more than memorized phrases spoken in a prescribed manner. Stimulating visitor enthusiasm and interest is the goal of the presentation; whether the goal is realized will be influenced greatly by style of presentation. Good teachers know that their attitudes influence student attitudes. Maintaining a high level of enthusiasm all day in a classroom can be demanding, but it is rewarding for both teacher and students. Similarly, in a museum, guides must sustain a high level of enthusiasm, for visitors deserve stimulating presentations.

We need to learn special techniques to involve our audiences, just as performing artists learn to project energy and draw in their audiences. The art of interpretation is comparable to any other performing art: skill in performance is acquired via experience, study, and observation. Guides, as interpreters, are the artists who make artifacts meaningful to visitors. The importance of the art of interpretation is described well by Lessinger and Gillis (1976):

> *Everything you wear, the house you live in, the cars you ride in—even the space capsule our astronauts went to the moon in—all of these were transferred from the abstraction of an idea into visualizations which enabled the abstract to be transformed into the real. Between the inventor and the manufacturer, there is an artist. Remember that, for we are living in a civilization which relies on art to act as the medium through which ideas are changed into objects. (p. 13)*

REHEARSAL

The techniques actors use in preparation for performances can serve guides successfully, too. Rehearsal is the most important activity for both performing artists and tour guides. Preparation of the material, planning of the techniques or activities to be used, and designing ways to move the group from place to place, are part of tour readiness and rehearsal. Rehearsal is essential for dealing with stage fright, a disease shared by beginning actors and beginning guides! The only handicap to a rehearsal is lack of an audience, because for actors and guides alike, the presence and response of an audience can be inspiring and motivating.

MENTAL REHEARSAL

Speaking, moving, and interacting with the group in one's imagination can be extremely helpful. It is possible to rehearse the entire tour, imagining reactions to various situations, problems that might arise, and answers to questions. Tour guides should begin by planning how a specific group will be greeted (visualize the group's size, average age, etc.). Nothing in the tour should be left to chance. How will the group be moved into the gallery? Will they sit or stand in a specific place? One should visualize the space. Has the tour been planned so that all can see and hear?

How will the discussion go—one should imagine talking and asking questions, waiting for responses, and how replies will be made. What activities have been planned? Are there instructions that should be given before the group moves at will? How will they be brought back together? If pencils and paper are used, will the group have directions for their use? We can imagine our facial expressions, posture, and gestures as we walk through the tour. Finally, how can group reactions be encouraged through improvements in our voice quality, gestures, and questions?

VERBAL REHEARSAL

An actual run-through of a tour, using questions, stories and all planned events, before friends or fellow docents (without an audience) is helpful. If the practice audience understands the rehearsal plan and offers advice, such a rehearsal of verbal material can be valuable. Often the performer-guide can only "come to life" when interacting with "real" visitors. There is no substitute for the inspiration and challenge of a live audience, eager for a satisfying experience in the museum setting. We learn quickly which verbal styles work best for us by touring many groups in a reasonably short amount of time. (Perhaps beginning guides would benefit if allowed to conduct tours frequently.) Practice audiences or observation of other guides is helpful, but they cannot substitute for first-hand experience.

Tour guides, however, should avoid memorizing the tour or presenting it verbatim to either their mock or real audiences. Rote presentations destroy rapport with a group and deny visitors spontaneity of interaction.

AUDIENCE INTERACTION

It is important for us to remember that touring involves interaction. Quality of interaction affects whether our interpretation is enthusiastic and whether visitors learn meaningfully at appropriate levels of understanding. To evaluate quality of interaction, tour guides must monitor visitors by watching their body language and facial expressions, by listening to their questions and comments, and by being flexible enough to alter aspects of the tour plan to meet their needs. "The mastery of content should be matched with an equal mastery of presentation" (Lessinger and Gillis, 1976, p. 14).

LEADERSHIP

Throughout our school years, teachers have traditionally assumed leadership roles. Visitors tend to treat guides similarly; they see them in charge of the group as knowledgeable "teachers." When leading groups, guides should accept the authority role willingly. If an audience perceives fear in a leader, the leader's credibility suffers. Fears common among most beginning guides must be put aside. Much of the anxiety among tour guides is due to self-doubt and insecurity about what the visitors will think of them. They may worry about how they look, whether they have enough information to answer questions, whether the group will prove hostile or restless, or how they will handle problems. Rehearsal is the best strategy for overcoming such fears and for gaining self-confidence.

Tour guides project their fears through the different ways in which they communicate with visitors. The worst aspect of fear is the inhibition it produces. Fear affects all aspects of delivery—voice, posture, memory, energy level, and so on, and guides should learn every technique possible for overcoming fears that might hinder a tour. Otherwise visitors may feel uncomfortable, which in turn, might ruin the museum experience for them.

SPACE AND DISTANCE

Visitors to museums, especially adults, usually stand six to eight feet away from the tour guide who is speaking to them. This "social" distance contributes to the image of the guide as a formal leader. It is a good idea to reduce the space between visitors and oneself by stepping forward two or three feet, for it is easier to make eye contact from closer range and to promote a sense of intimacy with the group. With groups of young children, tour guides can sit, kneel, or stand so that they can look directly into their eyes. It is also acceptable to touch younger children on the shoulder, especially when such gestures are part of one's personal style. Sometimes a light touch establishes personal contact and settles squirmy, inattentive youngsters.

When a group is seated, guides can move about freely, speaking to the group from many locations, but they must be careful not to obstruct the visitors' views of the collection. When groups disperse to look at an exhibit individually, guides might walk around to encourage visitors to ask questions that they might otherwise be reluctant to ask. Visitors find their museum experiences especially satisfying when they have opportunity for individual and group contact with guides.

TWO-WAY FEEDBACK

Feedback moves from visitors to guides and from guides to visitors. It can tell us, by a number of cues, how well we are doing in inspiring visitors and in communicating information to them. As we observe visitors during touring, we can note whether they seem critical of our delivery and style. Are they interested, or are they simply pretending to be interested? Do they appear distracted? Guides also can enhance their contact with audiences by offering them feedback. They should react with constructive, helpful responses to visitor questions and comments. Positive feedback reinforces visitors' interest in participating. People think that their questions and comments are of value and that they should be treated with respect.

VERBAL COMMUNICATION

Verbal communication is complex. As the guide thinks, thoughts are translated into words, and it is only the words that are communicated to visitors. The visitors, as listeners, in turn, consider the words and relate them to their experiences and knowledge. As straightforward as this seems, many disconnected areas of person-to-person communication may arise. Some common problems are listed below:

1. The presentation may not be organized properly or be offered in simple, clearly understood sentences.
2. The speaker and listeners may not share common understanding of either the subject or the words being used.
3. The listeners may fail to understand some of the words because they are pronounced incorrectly.
4. The speaker may express words and ideas too rapidly for the listeners to follow.
5. The listeners may not be able to hear.
6. The listeners may not be paying attention.

Guides should ask themselves, therefore, the following questions:

1. What are the characteristics of listeners for this tour?
2. Am I assuming too much knowledge on the part of the listeners?
3. What thoughts do I want to put into words?
4. Are my sentences easy for listeners to think about and understand?
5. Are my statements complete sentences?
6. Do the words I use say what I really mean?
7. Will my words mean something to the listeners?
8. Should I define any of the words in my sentence?
9. Will I pronounce all my words clearly and correctly?

SAYING WHAT WE MEAN

Today, unfortunately, many persons often mumble, abbreviate, and use repetitious, meaningless words and phrases. The result is often incomprehensible, disconnected, and ungrammatical. The frequent use of "you know," "er," "um," "like," and "basically" are disastrous for public speakers, but less offensive in personal conversation. Phrases like "I think" and "sort of" make it appear that the speaker is uncertain about facts. Catch words change often in the popular vernacular, and although these words demonstrate to young people the tour guide is "with it," they may confuse visitors in general. Furthermore, tour guides sometimes lose their train of thought in using unfamiliar, descriptive adjectives. A recent study, for example, found that as many as 28% of the respondents at an art lecture did not know the terms and concepts presented (Fischer, 1984). The lesson here is that, whenever possible, familiar words should be used.

SENTENCE STRUCTURE

Tour guides should think carefully about sentence structure. They might practice using complete, reasonably brief sentences that make their point precisely. Visitors find it more difficult to listen and translate words into meaning than to read and translate them into meaning. Written words can be read and re-read until they are understood. Practice is the best method for improving one's verbal communication skills. The best sentences are short.

When speaking, it is better for guides to work from an outline than a script. The presentation is likely to be more spontaneous. The outline encourages natural ways of speaking that reflect each tour guide's own personality. Rehearsal of the tour outline is essential in improving sentence structure. Taping several versions of the tour and listening to one's own sentences is especially helpful. Guides can think about what they want the visitor to know, and they can construct sentences accordingly. It is usually necessary to elaborate on various facts, and when sentences containing "nuggets" of information are brief and easily restated, visitors are more likely to remember the information. The interpretation of specific aspects of subject matter in the museum setting calls for specific, clearly stated sentences.

THE RIGHT WORDS

Although the tour outline may be carefully planned, guides should be as spontaneous as possible when speaking to visitors. Unpredictable circumstances often arise during open discussion, which may leave guides with a loss for words. Guides cannot know everything, and should not be afraid to say "I don't know." Naturally, memory can also fail, leaving guides without specific facts when they are needed. When a loss of words occurs, guides should admit it forthrightly in a normal, conversational manner. Fortunately, effective coping with the questions and comments of visitors increases with touring experience.

SPEAKING IN PUBLIC

Almost any voice can be developed and strengthened into a public speaking voice through practice in projection and enunciation. It is essential for guides to project (make the voice heard at a distance without yelling or changing its quality) so that the people in the back of a group can hear them. Nothing is more discouraging to visitors than to have to struggle to hear an interesting presentation. This problem is the primary reason that tour groups break up and drift away from their guides.

An appropriate voice level not only helps visitors stay interested; it can also help in controlling large or restless groups. Along with the quality of projection, however, tour guides need as well to change the pitch of their voices throughout the tour. Changing the tonal quality of the voice offers interesting variation, and prevents falling into a monotone, or speaking on the same "note," or level, all of the time. When there is a need to be emphatic, a voice change is important, as it causes people to become attentive.

It is helpful for tour guides to record their voices—to analyze critically projection, pitch, conversational habits, and overall quality. One might try reading conversationally from a book with some dialogue in it. Special qualities of one's voice, such as nasal tones, whining, or monotone tendencies, can be detected on recordings. Some women's voices are "light" or "high" in pitch. This is fine for conversation, but should be altered for projection. Tour guides should not be too harshly critical of themselves, however, because most of us do not find listening to our own voices very pleasant.

An interesting technique for using one's voice to keep a group's attention is to insert a rising inflection at the end of important sentences. This technique has been used by orators for many years and it is used effectively today by public speakers to sustain interest. It suggests that there is a comma at the end of the sentence and it draws people's attention to what is being said. It functions like a silent "and."

The following exercises are offered as helpful techniques tour guides might adopt for improving voice quality and projection. Such improvement also contributes to development of positive self-image.

Posture and the voice

When standing in a relaxed posture, one's feet should be slightly apart (aligned with the pelvic bones), knees relaxed, and weight slightly forward on the balls of the feet. (This requires flat shoes.) Weight should be evenly distributed on both feet. Weight distribution can be tested by "bouncing" lightly on the balls of the feet, keeping the knees flexed. One's rib cage should be elevated slightly, with shoulders back, but not strained, and arms hanging loosely at one's sides. This posture will improve voice quality, allow for better projection, and also will build self-confidence. Those who practice it can concentrate on the tour and forget how they "look," for good posture projects a positive image of personality. Problems to watch for: locked knees, weight unevenly distributed over one hip, slumped abdomen and chest, and head thrust forward. Not only will these affect voice quality, they may eventually cause physical discomfort.

Voice support

Practice contraction of the abdominal muscles (those that stretch horizontally and vertically across the abdomen and are attached to the back). One should pull in and tighten these muscles while breathing normally.

Breathing

While breathing, the diaphragm (near the upper abdomen, just under the rib cage) should go in and out. One's chest should not go up and down. (Singers learn to use the diaphragm for voice support and control.) When we sleep, we breathe naturally with the diaphragm. When only the lungs are used, the chest moves up and down in shorter, more frequent movements. When the diaphragm is used, air can be released slowly while talking, which means that more breath is available. A good test of proper breathing is to lie down, relax, and breathe normally. By placing one's hand just below the rib cage, one can practice breathing with the diaphragm. Soon it will be second nature.

Speaking

While breathing with the diaphragm and standing correctly, one should speak a sentence in a normal, conversational tone. Next, practice the same sentence by consciously lowering the voice and projecting it forcefully. We may think of this technique as "pushing" the voice, without shouting, toward either the back wall of the room or speaking to someone who is at a distance.

One should imagine that words are coming from the diaphragm rather than the mouth and that they are being "pushed" upward and outward. This exercise will produce a stronger, louder voice that can still fluctuate up and down in tone. This exercise should be practiced frequently in a variety of locations and surroundings—large open rooms or galleries, small carpeted areas, or out-of-doors. Acoustics may vary a great deal, even when going from one area to another in the same building, and delivery must be adjusted accordingly. Most institutions have periods of time during which visitors are not admitted. Staff and volunteers usually have access to the galleries and outside areas during these periods, and they may provide opportunities for rehearsing speaking skills.

Enunciation

In addition to sentence structure, guides should concentrate on enunciation (the art of pronouncing words clearly). Enunciation is important for two reasons: visitors need to **hear** what the guide is saying and to **understand** what the guide is saying. Hearing sounds and hearing words are not the same thing. The voice may carry well, but it doesn't help if enunciation is careless. In most instances, we fail to understand words because they are not clearly spoken rather than because they are not spoken loudly enough. Actors, public speakers, teachers and guides all must remember that clear pronunciation depends upon energetic use of the tongue and lips.

One might try reading a book aloud for the purpose of concentrating on the movements of the tongue and lips. In ordinary conversation we all suffer from "lazy tongue." We learn our native language as children, and this early training determines how we use our lips and tongues. Habits may be so strongly developed that we sometimes have trouble learning another language; we cannot easily change our speech habits to accommodate new combinations of sounds. Guides who are able to offer tours in another language may have to speak very slowly, unless they are extremely fluent. We might practice exaggerating lip and tongue movements while reading aloud. The exaggeration may feel strange at first, but if we watch ourselves in a mirror, we will not see unnatural contortions while we move our lips. Enunciation will improve noticeably; visitors, however, will not notice anything unusual.

Posture

Erect, attentive posture projects an image of leadership (see also the exercise, "Posture and the Voice"). Most of us tend to stand erect when in front of a group, perhaps the result of an inner voice from childhood admonishing us to stand up straight! We should approach a group confidently and purposefully, in a relaxed manner, and greet visitors with a smile. (Holding one's arms loosely at the sides indicates an openness to others.) We might anticipate how we would greet guests in our homes and adopt the same tone of voice and gestures. A calm, assured attitude is best; after all, we are "at home" in the museum setting, and we want to make visitors feel comfortable and welcome.

Tour guides are expected to be leaders and to be responsible for everything that happens during the tour. However, it is important not to present an authoritarian stance that threatens visitors—especially small ones. Leaders can be polite, sympathetic, friendly and approachable and still be in charge of groups. As a tour progresses, a guide should avoid leaning or slumping against walls, doorways, or exhibition structures. It can be disconcerting to watch a tour guide shift constantly from one posture to another; moreover, it seems to give visitors permission to behave similarly.

Jokes, ethnic comments, sexist remarks

Tour guides should choose humorous anecdotes or jokes carefully. Children are particularly sensitive to cynicism and have difficulty coping with it. Jokes and cynical remarks at someone's expense occur all too often in classrooms. Considering the cross-section of people who travel and visit museums, it is important to avoid making any seemingly prejudicial statements or derogatory comments about minorities or other cultures. A tour guide should never indicate that the European or American culture is superior in any way. This may seem obvious advice to anyone who speaks in public, but sometimes we are oblivious to our offensive remarks. Sometimes sensitivity to others is all that is needed. A good way to test for prejudicial implications in a presentation is to remove oneself completely from it and attempt to look at one's words and attitudes objectively. The worst offenses, however, may occur when comments are spontaneous. Guides should treat every group politely and equally. They must be careful to avoid unwarranted assumptions about anyone's background and occupation, relationships of visitors to each other, and shared values, beliefs, and tastes. They must not assume that only a certain type or class or people will enjoy or understand exhibits; such stereotyping inhibits efforts to reach out to the entire community.

Sexist remarks are especially offensive. Unfortunately, many of us are also oblivious to the sexist comments we make. For example, we sometimes forget that the traditional family unit is a minority and many women are heads of households. Over 50% of today's workers are women, and an equally high percentage of women are now the sole supporters of their families. Women as well as men are mathematicians, doctors, stock brokers, lawyers and owners of businesses in our modern society. Women are particularly proud of the progress that they have made in many aspects of society and of the recognition that they have received in the past two decades for their abilities and contributions. An unconscious slight of women, an implication that men possess the more influential and dominant sex in our society, or a suggestion that men more than women can understand "technical" subjects, may set the wrong mood for a tour. For example, a female guide was heard to say "I don't know how this works, could one of the men in the group explain it to us?" What happens when visitors offer tasteless jokes or make ethnic or sexist remarks? It is difficult to predict what form these remarks might take. Sometimes they can be ignored, but it is always wise to have a few prepared responses ready. A polite rebuttal, "Well, not all of us agree with your viewpoint" may be satisfactory.

THE ARGUMENTATIVE VISITOR

Simple responses to an argumentative visitor are always more effective than arguing at length to prove who is right. Guides should offer a brief, simple reaction ("Perhaps historical facts prove otherwise."), or suggest a specific source of information ("I recently read about that in ________ , and I found it helpful. You might enjoy it, too."), and move right on to another topic. However, there may be times when it is better to be unresponsive and move along. Most visitors will make incorrect statements unintentionally, but occasionally someone deliberately wants to start an argument or continue a disagreement at length with either the guide or members of the group. Such people cannot be convinced in a few minutes that they are out of line. Other members of a group usually feel embarrassed along with the guide, and they are glad to change the subject. Each circumstance will be unique, but with a little experience, a tour guide should have little difficulty fending off an argumentative visitor.

NONVERBAL COMMUNICATION: WHAT WE DON'T SAY

"Nonverbal communication is a basic, primitive form of conveying information from one person to another. It has been estimated that in a normal conversation between two people, only one-third of the meaning is transmitted on a verbal level, and nearly two-thirds on a nonverbal level" (Brill, 1973, p. 36). To have the meaning of a tour understood completely requires using nonverbal communication skills well—body language, gestures, and facial expressions. Guides can inspire enthusiasm and can involve visitors with an exhibit by nonspoken communication as well as oral delivery. During the tour, it is important that nonverbal communication be congruent with the verbal presentation.

A great deal of personal interaction has to do with nonverbal communication skills. First the environment of the institution conveys messages about comfort or discomfort to visitors that may be with them for their entire visit. Second, "silent" messages from the interpreter support or interfere with the meaning of the presentation. Guides "talk" to people through facial expressions, eye contact, gestures, voice, touch, ways they move their bodies, appearance (clothing and jewelry), and physical proximity. What kind of message, for example, is communicated when guides are late for a tour and visitors are kept waiting? Obviously, visitors are being told that something other than the tour has higher priority.

Every culture has unwritten rules of body language that are understood by others in that culture. Smiling, crying, and other facial expressions are generally universal. When touring visitors from other countries, tour guides cannot be certain that the visitors understand familiar forms of nonverbal communication. Even within the United States, people who grew up in the East may behave somewhat differently from Westerners. Those who live in cities exhibit slightly different behavior from people who come from rural areas. City dwellers, for example, are accustomed to carrying on their daily activities in the midst of large numbers of people, whether shopping, eating meals in restaurants, driving in traffic, or engaging in recreation. Predominant clothing colors differ from region to region depending on climate. When we are speaking with family members or close friends in private conversation, we may assume that they have the same background of knowledge and experience that we have, and therefore, we know much of what we communicate to one another is intuitive and unspoken. In tours, however, we cannot make these assumptions. We must be conscious of our nonverbal expressions in order to ensure that they convey the meaning that we intend.

BODY LANGUAGE

Interpreters can evaluate how well the tour is proceeding by observing the visitors' body language. For example, people may show rejection by folding their arms or moving or turning away (Scheflen, 1964). Students may be restless when they move about or whisper. Sometimes, however, the museum environment restricts the behavior of visitors. It calls for relative quiet to enable people to look at exhibits and read labels; therefore, visitor reaction may be subdued and difficult to diagnose. People often believe that they should not express their feelings in such a setting. Students sometimes stand ill at ease and appear disinterested because of the unfamiliar environment, the presence of a guard, or an overbearing adult. (Contrast the demand for a quiet environment with a hands-on science museum, rock concert, or sporting event where conversation and enthusiasm are encouraged.) Docents should establish allowable behavior with visitors at the outset, and, if possible, encourage natural conversation and discussion.

The private distance which people establish around themselves is called "personal space." It is a barrier of different dimensions. Although there is some variation world-wide, generally four distances are relatively significant everywhere.

1. **intimate**—under 18 inches—this is the distance we use for lovemaking, close friends and relatives, and with children.
2. **personal**—divided in two parts—a close personal (18-30 inches) and far personal (2½ to 4 feet)—within these zones we deal with persons whom we know well.
3. **social**—4 to 12 feet—this is the distance we use for relatively formal or business communications.
4. **public**—beyond 12 feet—the distance we maintain with strangers except in buses, elevators, and tour groups, where it must be disregarded. However, strangers in close proximity will establish their own private space by standing quietly, being careful not to touch anyone, and not looking into anyone's eyes (Sielski, 1979).

Interpreters work usually within the social distance category of 4 to 12 feet. When the distance goes much beyond ten or twelve feet, eye contact may be interrupted for too long, and guides risk "losing" the group. Guides thus should take care not to move away from a group of visitors too quickly.

FEAR CAN BE CONCEALED

Fear while guiding tours is generally called "stage fright"—the nervous condition that precedes any public appearance. Seasoned artists and guides often suffer from stage fright, but the minute that they are "on stage" before an audience, all goes wonderfully well. To some extent, this nervous condition may help promote a rush of adrenaline that actually will enliven the presentation. The energy generated by fear can be redirected positively to style and delivery. One way we can overcome fear is to know so much about a subject that we are not afraid of running out of things to say. Another remedy for fear is to become so interested in visitor questions and responses that we forget our self-consciousness. Also, tour guides who practice communication skills will find that the overwhelming symptoms of fear become manageable or disappear in time.

Acting skills can help disguise fear also. Children are very good at playing "let's pretend." Adults can "pretend," too, when faced with unusual and difficult situations. They may simply carry on as though they knew what they were doing. A firm grasp of the material for the tour and several practice sessions will alleviate feelings of panic. Guides soon learn that they really do know more about the subject at hand than most visitors, who, for the most part, are eager and willing participants in the tour.

PERSONAL IMAGERY

People judge each other by appearances, so we try to project favorable images to others. It is possible to alter one's projected image through changes in body movements and dress. However, body language cannot overcome lack of concern for the visitors. If we do not truly enjoy talking to strangers, the quality of the tour will be compromised. We need to be ourselves, polite, honest, unaffected, and natural, as well as aware of the unspoken messages we communicate. We should enjoy meeting people and exchanging ideas. Sincere enthusiasm for the subject and for the museum is important element in successful touring.

Arms, Hands, and Gestures. Arm movements ought to be used sparingly and naturally. The most comfortable and natural way to hold hands and arms is at one's side. Sometimes it is helpful to clasp them loosely in front of one's body. Those who like to put their hands in their pockets should try doing so one hand at a time. Having both hands jammed into one's pockets appears as a nervous gesture, whereas having only one hand loosely in a pocket conveys relaxation.

Tour guides should use sweeping arm gestures or pointing sparingly and only when the discussion requires such action. When specific, hard to see areas are being talked about, pointing carefully directs attention toward them. (In art museums, pointing is especially discouraged because of the potential hazard to art objects.) When discussing a free-standing object, sweeping gestures can be avoided by standing in a position that allows visitors appropriate access to it. If pointing is necessary, hands should be kept at least twelve inches from the object. Flashlights with arrows of light are the most satisfactory pointers. Tour guides must not touch objects if the museum has rules that visitors are not to touch them. When tour guides are allowed to handle an art object, gloves should be worn to protect the object and to convey the "no touching" rule.

Guides should not have to look at objects in order to talk about them. They should point only occasionally at specific areas. They should stand so that visitors can easily see the objects under discussion. If folders, baskets of materials, or any other objects are to be used as part of the tour, they should be placed in areas where they are to be used before the tour begins. Guides should not carry objects or papers, including purses, in their hands during a tour.

Laughter. Laughing together breaks down barriers. Finding a joke or comment that helps the guide and group laugh together early in the tour establishes rapport and friendship. There is a certain innocence in laughter—children laugh easily, but adults often need to be coaxed. (See "Jokes, Ethnic Comments, and Sexist Remarks earlier in this chapter.)

Eye Contact. Eye contact is probably one of the most important and influential factors in establishing rapport with an individual or group. When welcoming the tour group, it is best to make eye contact with most individuals right away by slowly looking from one person to another, hesitating slightly at each person, and smiling while talking. (Students may feel somewhat uncomfortable with eye contact.) Direct, personal contact will produce a one-to-one relationship with visitors. The sense of friendship and familiarity will encourage visitors to ask questions and make comments. There may be several occasions during the tour when the tour guide makes sweeping eye contact.

When talking to a group at large, should direct eye contact be disconcerting at first, tour guides may try looking just over the tops of heads in the back row, moving their eyes from one head to another. This technique gives the appearance at least of eye contact. As confidence grows in the content and format of the tour, guides can begin making actual eye contact with individuals. Direct eye contact, in any case, is essential for question and answer formats. Guides must be careful to share attention throughout the group, not giving too much attention to one or two visitors. Eye contact also is helpful in drawing a visitor's attention back to the discussion.

Clothing. Personal appearance is important. How we look tells people how we feel about ourselves and about the institution we represent, even before the tour begins. The most important aspect of clothing is that it not be distracting. Guides should not be overdressed, or dressed in such an extreme style that the museum objects are less attention-getting than the guide's appearance! Jewelry can be distracting, too, if it is excessive. Both clothing and jewelry can be worn to advantage, however, if they complement or illustrate the exhibits. Some guides wear Native American jewelry, shirts, woven sashes, or scarves as examples of cultural art and decoration. Or, they may wear costumes of a historical period to illustrate some aspect of an exhibit. These can all be very effective when carried out in moderation.

The color of a tour guides' clothing can help or hinder a tour in an art museum. If we wish to emphasize color in paintings, it might be advisable to wear a solid color that will demonstrate some color property. If color is not significant, colors in clothing which are highly intense will be distractive. In open settings, or when large groups are toured, we may wish to wear brightly colored shirts, jackets, or caps in order to be seen easily. European tour guides, for example, often carry red umbrellas! Some museums prefer that guides wear uniforms or an article of clothing that serves as an identifying symbol. Clothing should be, above all, comfortable. It is essential that we are able to relax without concern for our appearance. Neatness, in this case, is more important than fashion. Feeling good about our outward appearance allows the inner self to function more efficiently.

The same basic characteristics of touring or teaching hold for both children and adults. Above all, thoughtfulness and politeness should be the most important personal qualities of tour guides. They must not be blatantly authoritarian, but still they must be in charge. Content should unfold steadily. Tour guides should be certain that everyone understands as the presentation ensues. In addition to tour techniques, content, and vocal skills, guides should give thought to maintaining nonverbal interaction with visitors. Smiles, shared laughter, and steady eye contact are essential with children and adolescents and important with adults (Fines, 1982). Guides should be poised and self-confident; they should model excellent speaking skills and grammar. All these stylistic considerations and interpersonal skills are important, for the overall appearance, knowledge, and personal style of tour guides affects visitors' willingness to participate in museum learning experiences.

REFERENCES

Brill, N. T. (1973). **Working with People.** New York: J. B. Lippincott.

Fines, J. (1982). Imagination in teaching—reflections on my fortnight's work. **Roundtable Reports: The Journal of Museum Education,** 7(2), 3-10.

Fischer, D. K. (1984). New data from old masters. **Museum Studies Journal, 1**(3), 36-50.

Lessinger, L., & Gillis, D. (1976). **Teaching as a Performing Art.** Dallas, Texas: Crescendo Publications, Inc.

Scheflen, A. E. (1964). The significance of posture in communication systems. **Psychiatry, 7,** 316-331.

Sielski, L. M. (1979). Understanding body language. **Personnel and Guidance Journal, 57,** 238-242.

Winner, T. (1984). **Literature and the creative process.** In Colloquia on Creativity: Two views of Semiotics, sponsored by the Philosophy of Education Research Center at the Harvard Graduate School of Education, Cambridge, Massachusetts.

CHAPTER EIGHT
Putting it All Together

The earliest museums in America began as private collections. In the United States, the first public museums opened late in the 18th century in Charleston, South Carolina, and in Philadelphia, Pennsylvania. No one then thought to adapt the early museums to educational functions. Public education in museums, as we know it, progressed slowly through the years. It took almost one hundred and fifty years for museums to acknowledge their educational responsibilities to society. And when they did, few, if any, administrators either recognized or promoted the potential of museum education. Gradually, educational interpretations of exhibits began to improve through more informative labels. Then, early in the twentieth century, the first docent programs for touring the public were established in Boston and New York City.

Museum educators are now developing diverse programs and interpretive tours. And recent technological advances—video machines, projectors, and cassette players—have added new dimensions to interpretation. Exhibit design has also improved greatly. Museum exhibits today cover all facets of museum offerings, from ancient to modern, and they are displayed in attractive, appealing ways.

Two subtle attitude shifts in our society have affected contemporary museums. The first change stems from recognition of the contributions ethnic groups have made to cultural heritage in the United States. This awareness has led to the establishment of a number of museums which preserve the art and artifacts of major ethnic groups. Highly interesting and more varied museum collections are thus available for enjoyment and study. The second change follows from intensified efforts by museums to collect and preserve the art and artifacts that represent the history of the United States. Objects that were once overlooked or deemed unimportant are now carefully preserved and displayed. Many unknown and superb collections of such objects are coming to light. Community museums also have begun actively to chronicle the history of regional areas.

Museums increasingly are surveying visitors to learn more about their audiences. They are displaying unusual exhibitions and presenting new programs to attract people who have never visited museums. They know that social change will affect program focus in the future, and they are taking note of the new interests and lifestyles of citizens.

Museum visitors may be of all ages and from all social and ethnic backgrounds. Of course, the predominant visitor type will vary with the museum. Children's museums and science and technology centers, for example, attract mostly children and families. Art museums have more adult visitors. Each museum group, including people brought together incidentally, however, has certain characteristics in common, and it is this commonality within groups that makes accurate preplanning possible.

Planning a tour is not an easy task; many different components must be considered in its preparation. Tour guides must know the characteristics of visitors who frequent their museum and, for each general grouping of them, the most effective tour technique. Also, interpreters must be aware of their own personal styles, and they must understand ways of correcting problems that might interfere with the tour presentation. An important aspect of successful museum tour planning is that of studying and perfecting style of presentation. Information can be presented more effectively after attention to verbal and nonverbal techniques of communication, including good voice projection, attention to posture, sensitivity to the people in the group, and so forth. By taking these concerns into consideration, guides will thus grow in confidence and knowledge, and at the same time, develop the social skills for giving better tours.

The challenge of providing "real" learning in the museum setting raises many issues still open to debate. Although considerable research and study will be necessary to come up with definitive answers, we are convinced that the most meaningful way to view objects and exhibits is through guided tours. Effective guides become intermediary, educational specialists between the exhibits and the visitors. Tour guides who bring to their responsibilities high levels of professionalism and enthusiasm will present excellent tours.

Museum visitors are always learning in some way. However, the quantity and quality of their learning is dependent, in part, upon the tour guides' efforts. Tour guides thus must become acquainted with how people learn. Concepts of learning may seem difficult, and there is the temptation to ignore them. Tour guides who are aware of visitor capabilities for learning, however, can heighten the meaningfulness of museum visits. The learning and development viewpoints that impact most directly on museum learning center on how persons at different ages integrate and deal with their museum experiences and how persons at different ages relate to one another socially. When tour guides present information to visitors at appropriate levels of intellectual and social understanding, the new knowledge may produce attitude change, and hopefully, new, more enlightened ways of dealing with situations outside the museum.

Our understanding of children's intellectual growth reveals that they shift from concrete to abstract thinking as they mature, that is, from specific, somewhat unrelated thoughts to general, integrative concepts. Opportunities to manipulate and handle objects, which many museums provide, help growing children find more effective relationships among things in their environments. As young people move through successive stages of intellectual and social development, they will think, reason, and relate to other persons differently. And how well people of different ages understand the museum exhibits will depend upon their levels of maturity. Tour guides must be aware of developmental levels at the different stages of growth so that they may adapt tour techniques and subject-matter content appropriately.

The Good Guide emphasizes three tour techniques that the experiences of tour guides have shown to be highly successful.

The Lecture-Discussion technique presents information within an instructional format. Opportunity for discussion is limited. The effectiveness of this tour technique is dependent upon a knowledgeable and skillful lecturer; moreover, it is not appropriate for all visitor groups.

The Inquiry-Discussion technique stresses "discussion" in which guides and visitors participate throughout the tour. Questions are used to direct discussion toward the fulfillment of tour objectives. They are used to promote visitor thinking, questioning, and answering at different levels of complexity. The most important aspect of the inquiry technique in tours is its potential for stimulating thinking at higher and higher conceptual levels. A sequence of questions regarding objects might proceed from concrete to abstract as follows:

name them . . .
describe their attributes . . .
classify them with other objects which have similar attributes . . .
think about other ways the objects could be used . . .
infer or project possibilities . . .
evaluate the objects for their technical, aesthetic, and cultural

qualities . . .

The Guided Discovery technique tailors the tour to visitors' individual interests and intellectual levels. Visitors, particularly students, respond to the stimulation of the discovery tour method because they have opportunity to seek information that intrigues them. Interest is sustained throughout the tour. Another advantage of learning by Guided Discovery is that the experiences of learning are nonthreatening to self-esteem.

Each of the three major tour techniques enables guides to focus on both Object-Directed and Object-Associated exhibit information. Object-Directed content is concerned solely with the object, in and of itself. Object-Associated information, in contrast, relates objects to cultural, historical, and personal contexts. We argue that it is preferable to increase the number of ways visitors look at objects; therefore, we advocate always including Object-Associated information during a tour. Visitors need object associations and references; they increase the ways that visitors "see" exhibits.

Our view is that tour guides should plan tours by keeping insights drawn from learning theories generally in mind and knowledge regarding museum exhibits specifically in mind. After finding out about the characteristics of a group soon to visit the museum, guides may consult **The Good Guide** for information about how to deal with these characteristics during a tour. If it is a student group, for example, guides must determine its members intellectual and social levels of learning. When the tour material is presented properly, it will be an important factor in the tour's success and, of course, it will be crucial to how well group members understand and retain the tour content.

Visitor characteristics influence how available knowledge about exhibits is to be presented, which in turn, affects choice of a tour technique. If a tour subject has been chosen, the manner of presentation of the tour is critical. For example, if group members wish to view a particular exhibit that has been highly publicized, they may prefer to see specific pieces in the collection. Perhaps, because of time limitations, guides may choose to select a few pieces that are representative, combine Object-Associated and Object-Directed discussion, and let the group members tour individually after part of the allotted tour time has passed. Visitors, therefore, will have been given both the skills to "see" each object and the associations that make the objects meaningful. When a subject has not been preselected, inquiry, including fairly structured questioning and discussion, may help determine special interests. However, the first task for the tour guide, before object selection, is to choose the objectives and the learning goals of the tour. They provide the intellectual route by which the tour proceeds and by which special interests may be integrated into the tour.

We emphasize, for all varieties of tour, that interaction between guide and visitors ensures a more interesting and responsive tour. Inter-

TABLE FOUR

TOUR PLANNING GUIDE

DATE OF TOUR ______

GROUP ______

CONTACT ______
Telephone ______

AUDIENCE TYPE ______

Characteristics ______
______

Spec. Learning
Characteristics ______

EXHIBIT OR SUBJECT ______
_ Request

INTERPRETIVE TECHNIQUE ______

(Alternate Methods) ______

OBJECTIVE(S) ______
______

Learning Goals ______
______

Key Questions (Inquiry-Discussion) ______

"Problems" (Discovery) ______
______
______

Other: _ Object-Assoc.
_ Object-Direct.
_ Theme ______

AIDS OR SUPPORTING ACTIVITIES ______
______

OBJECTS SELECTED	IMPORTANT FACTS

SAMPLE TOUR PLANNING GUIDE

DATE OF TOUR	October 16, 1986
GROUP	Rural School (Grade: 5)
CONTACT	John Smith
Telephone	123-4567
AUDIENCE TYPE	Older Children, 8-11
Characteristics	Allow interaction, literal minded; socialized
Spec. Learning Characteristics	present & concrete; cause & effect
EXHIBIT OR SUBJECT	History of community
x Request	
INTERPRETIVE TECHNIQUE	Inquiry-Discussion
(Alternate Methods)	Guided Discovery
OBJECTIVE(S)	Students will see four aspects of 19th cent. coastal village life.
Learning Goals	Compare and contrast four examples of commerce: select 3 objects of each.
Key Questions (Inquiry-Discussion)	Name, group, inference questions.
"Problems" (Discovery)	Shipbuilding, fishing, business, agriculture: Similarities, etc.; have students document.
Other: x Object-Assoc.	
x Object-Direct.	
_ Theme	No
AIDS OR SUPPORTING ACTIVITIES	10 min. slide show; data-retrieval, storytelling.

OBJECTS SELECTED	IMPORTANT FACTS
Lighthouse model	interactive, built in 18xx_
Clipper ship models	illustrates trade, technology.

action also moves people intellectually from one point to another—to increasing levels of complexity regarding the tour's content.

An example of tour planning, which is based upon insights presented in **The Good Guide,** is illustrated with a group of fifth graders, about 10 to 11 years of age, in the Sample Tour Planning Guide represented below. We find from Table One (Chapter Three) that the primary intellectual characteristic that affects learning at this age level is involvement with concrete experiences. However, fifth-graders are also beginning to reason inductively and to understand cause and effect relations. They are beginning, too, to understand the social perspectives of others and to make inferences about them. (For more thorough understanding of this visitor group, and many others, tour guides should refer to the detailed information presented in Chapter Three, [How People Learn] and Chapter Six [Audiences: Who's Listening?].) Given the intellectual and social development of fifth-graders, one objective has been chosen for the group, and learning goals have been selected to help attain the objective. Next, we prepared key questions regarding the objective and learning goals. After these decisions were reached, tour aids were chosen from a number of activities. Some of these, however, may be left out during the actual tour to allow more time for questioning, discovery, problem solving, and discussion.

The best tour technique for a group of fifth graders, in our judgement, is either the Inquiry-Discussion or the Guided Discovery. As the Sample Tour Planning Guide shows, we have chosen the Inquiry-Discussion for this particular group. We note also that their classroom teacher has requested a tour that will deal with the history of the community. For purposes of illustration, we assume that the school is located in a northeastern coastal community; therefore, as guides, we plan to compare and contrast four types of commerce during the historical period we consider. Thus, we cover shipbuilding, agriculture, fishing and lobstering, and local pharmacy trade. Our hypothetical tour plan includes support for the tour presentation in the way of a brief slide show, a true story about a sea captain, and some data-retrieval packets that will be useful both in the museum and in the classroom following the field trip.

Readers are encouraged to make blank forms of Table 4, the Tour Planning Guide, and to use them in developing tour outlines of their own. The Tour Planning Guide, is, of course, only an outline; objectives, learning goals, and questions would be developed in considerably greater detail for an actual tour.

The content of **The Good Guide** is derived from the premise that the museum experience is different from all others. Its advantage is the physical presence of rare and unique objects. Guided tours supplement and extend label information about exhibits of these objects. Interpreters create the best possible tour when they integrate what they know about visitors, what they know about the museum exhibits, and importantly, what they know about tour planning. We are convinced that effective touring is based on linking museum objects to **meaningful** facts. Furthermore, it is equally critical that objects or groups of objects be related both to cultural and social contexts and to personal experiences. Learning will not occur unless relationships developed in the museum are meaningful in the visitors' lives. Visitors also need more than single kinds of experiences during a tour—those that are intellectual, which pertain to knowledge, and those that are affective, which deal with attitudes and emotions—are both significant. We believe, therefore, that tour guides should acquire background knowledge about visitor groups and should present tours that integrate objects and exhibits. Tour guides are there to help visitors achieve successful, meaningful learning experiences and to help museums fulfill their responsibilities to society.

INDEX

Abstract
  art, 27
  objective, 53
  questions, 73
  thinking, 27
Activities, Tour, 68, 69, 79
Adam, T. R., 14
Adolescents, 97-102
  and Piaget, 30
  motivating, 101-102
Adult education, in museums, 13
Adults
  as tour members, 105
  as volunteers, 4
  crystallized intelligence, 105
  fluid intelligence, 105
  senior, 106-107
  young, 104, 105
Affective domain, 22, 24, 25, 26
Affective learning, 22, 25
American Association of Museums, 14, 20
American Council for the Arts, 91
Andrews, K., 101
Ashmolean Museum, 11
Astor, Caroline, 44
Audiences
  characteristics of, 98, Table II
  definition of, 91-92
  interaction with, 120
  see also Groups; Visitors
Audio-tours, 45
Audio-visual aids, 80

Balling, J. D., 43
Barlow, G. C., 112
Bay, A. I., 13, 15
Bettleheim, B., 35
Booth, J. H., 15
Boston Children's Museum, 15
Boston Museum of Fine Arts, 12, 19
Brill, N. T., 128
Brooklyn Museum, 101
Bruner, J., 36

California Palace of the Legion of Honor, 70
Carnegie Foundation, 14
Children
  and tours, 92-97, 136
  stages of cognitive development, 29-31
  and imagination, 48, 49
  characteristics of, Tables I, II
Cognitive
  domain, 22, 24, 26
  learning, 28
  definition of, 27
  development, 28-29
  Piaget's four stages of, 29-31
  school, 27-28
Commission on Museums for a New Century, 15, 20
Communication, 117
  eye contact, 131
  feedback, 122
  jokes, ethnic, sexist remarks, 126
  laughter in, 131
  nonverbal, 128
  public speaking skills, 122-126
  rehearsal for, 119-120
  space and distance, 121, 129
  verbal, 122
Comparison and contrast, 48
Concept formation, 27-28, 31
  examples of, 27

Concrete
  objectives, 53
  questions, 73
  thinking, 29
Conservation, need for, 16
Convergent questions, 73
Cultural pluralism, 14, 20
Curators, and guides, 6

Dana, J. C., 12-13, 14
Dewey, J., 15, 37-38
Discovery learning, 28, 35
Discovery tours
  in Great Britain, 17, 66-67
  see also Guided Discovery
Divergent questions, 74
Docent, *see* Guides
Domains, learning, 22, 24-26

Early adolescence, 97-99
Early childhood, 93-94
Edwards, Y., 10
Eisner, E. W., 24
Environments, new, and students, 43
Ethnic Groups, *see* Minorities
Exhibitions
  "blockbuster," 17
  labeling of, 14, 19
  traveling, 16-17
  visitor interaction with, 17
Exploratorium, The, 15, 70

Falk, J. M., 43
Family group, 109-110
Faneuil Hall, Boston, 47
Fear, concealment of, 129
Feldman, E. B., 47
Films, 80
Fines, J., 47, 132
Fischer, D. K., 123
Foreign visitors, cultural differences, 115
Formal learning, 45-46

Gagne, R. M., 23, 24, 36, 75
Games, tour, 78
Gardner, H., 100
Gifted student, 102-103
Gillis, D., 55, 119, 120
Gilman, B. I., 12, 14, 19
Glaser, R., 36
Graburn, N. H. H., 20, 41, 43
Groups
  adolescent, 100-102
  adult, 105-106
  characteristics of, Table II
  definition, 91
  early adolescent, 99-99
  early childhood, 93-94
  family, 109-110
  foreign, 115
  gifted student, 102-103
  handicapped, 112-114
  large, 84
  logistics, 83
  minority, 110-112
  mixed ages, 102-115
  older children, 96-97
  organization, 83-85
  random, 71
  rapport with, 82-83
  school age, 92-102
  senior adults, 106-107
  young adults, 104-105
  young children, 94-95
  see also Audiences; Visitors
Guided Discovery, 63-70, 137
  definition of, 63
  objectives and learning goals, 67-68
  outline, 67-70
  tour recommendations for, Table II
  visitor control in, 67
Guided Involvement, 71
Guides
  and communication, 6
  and school groups, 65-67, 91
  and staff, 6-7
  as performers, 119
  as teachers, 5
  definition of, 3
  expectations of, 7
  in museums, 19
  program, earliest, 12, 19
  responsibilities of, 8-9
  rewards to, 8
  training of, 4, 7

Handicapped visitors, 112-114
  definition of, 112
  federal regulation 504, 112
  hearing impairment, 113
  learning disabilities, 114
  mental retardation, 114
  speech, language impairment, 112
  visual disabilities, 113
Heard Museum, The, 6
Hicks, E. C., 20
Hispanics, 20
Horn, A., 70-71
Hudson, K., 15

Ianotti, R. J., 35
Igoe, K., 35
Improvisation, 78
Indianapolis Museum, 101
Informal learning, 43-45
Information processing, 31-35
  and social cognition, 32
  definition of, 31
Inquiry-Discussion, 60-63, 78, 81, 84, 136
  definition of, 60
  outline for, 60-63
  tour recommendations for, Table II
  versus lecture-discussion, 63
Interactive exhibits, 80-81
Interpretation
  as interaction, 18-19
  definition of, 9-10
  labels for, 14, 18
Interpreter, *see* Guides
Interpretive techniques, 56-72
  Guided Discovery, 63-70
  Inquiry-Discussion, 60-63
  Lecture, 70-71
  Lecture-Discussion, 57-59

Judgemental questions, 74

Keislar, E., 37
Keppel, F. E., 14, 15
Klausmeier, H., 36
Knowles, M. S., 105

Labels
  didactic, 42
  exhibit, 14, 18
Laetsch, W. M., 109
Lanier, V., 43
Learning
  active involvement in, 23, 48
  by discovery, 35-37
  cognitive school, 27-28
  definition of, 24
  domains, 22, 24-26
  goals, 54, 55
  methods for tours, 48
  overview, 22
  structures, 43-46
  through tours, 38
  to teach, 5
  two descriptions of, 26
Learning focus, 46
  object-associated, 47-48, 137
  object-directed, 46-47, 137
Lecture tours, 70-71
Lecture-Discussion, 57-59, 78, 84, 136
  definition of, 57
  outline for, 58-60
  versus Inquiry-Discussion, 63
Lehman, S. M., 35
Lessinger, L., 55, 119, 120
Levels of questions, 74
  classifying and grouping objects, 75
  discriminating characteristics, 74
  evaluation and judgement, 76
  making inferences, 75
  naming objects, 74
Levinson, B., 86

Madeja, S. S., 47
Marcouse, R., 17
Marsh, C., 77
Martin, W. W., 43
Materials, hands-on, 78-79
Memory questions, 73
Minorities, 110-112
  contributions, 14
  ethnic comments about, 126,127
  population of, 20
Moore, E. M., 4
Motor domain, 22

Multicultural education, in Great Britain, 17
Munley, M. E., 20
Museum education
 as a priority, 15
 future of, 19-20
 in other countries, 17
 and schools, 4
Museums
 and children, 17
 and education, 14, 15-16
 and John Dewey, 37-38
 and interpretation, 18-19
 and schools, 17-18, 92-93
 conservation in, 16-17
 funding in, 16
 urban, 13
 participatory activities, 17
 early influence of, 12
 public, 12
Museums, learning in
 barriers to, 41
 environment for, 41, 42
 exhibits as a source for, 42
 formal, 45-46
 informal, 43-45
 self-guided, 40-41
 stimulation for, 42
 tour methods, 48
Muuss, R. E., 32, 35

National Commission on Resources for Youth, 97
National Arts and Handicapped Information Service, 114
National Research Center of the Arts, 90
Newsom, B. Y., 13, 19
Nonverbal communication
 personal space, 129
 fear, 129
 personal imagery, 130
 body language, 129

O'Connell, P., 101
Object-Associated tours, 46, 47-48, 56, 136
 questions, 62
Object-Directed tours, 46-47, 56, 136
 questions, 62
Object-oriented tours, 47
Objectives
 abstract, concrete, 53
 tour, 52-55
Objects, 41
 learning focus for, 46-47
 selecting, 55
Old Sturbridge Village, 15, 20, 44
Oppenheimer, F., 70
Outline preparation, 52-55

Pavlov, I., 26
Peale, C. W., 12
Piaget, J., 15, 23, 28-29, 75
 implications of theory, 31
 object permanence, 14, 29
 stages of cognitive development, 29-31, Table I
Plimoth Plantation, 44

Questions
 encouraging, 77
 from notebook, 56
 levels of, 74-76
 open-ended, 59, 75-76
 strategies for, 72-77
 types of, 73-74
 visitor response to, 72
 from visitors, 77
 waiting for answers to, 76-77

Random tours, 71
Reasoning, definition of, 27
Rehearsal
 verbal, 120
 mental, 119
Richardson, E., 12
Roessel, R. A., 111

S-R School, *see* Stimulus-Response
Sample Tour Planning Guide, 139
Samples, R., 75
Scheflen, A. E., 129
Schlereth, T., 44
 and conceptual models, 47-48
School Council, 66
Schools
 and museums, 17-18

groups from, 52
guided discovery and, 65-67
Selman, R.
five stages of social cognition, 32-34, Table I
Shulman, L. S., 37
Sielski, L. M., 129
Silver, A. Z., 12, 13, 19
Skill domain, *see* Motor
Skinner, B. F., 26
Social cognition
and information processing, 32
definition of, 32
and children's emotions, 34
and children's perspective, 34, 35
Staff, museum, 6-7, 42
early training, 13
relationships with guides, 6
nineteenth century, 13
Stanley, J. C., 104
Stimulus-Response school, 26
Storytelling, 78, 79
Style, personal
clothing, 131
posture, 126
voice, 124

Thematic emphasis for tours, 49
Thompson, B., 47
Thorndike, E. L., 26
Tilden, F., 19
Tomkins, C., 12
Tours
aids for, 78
background materials for, 55
conceptual models for, 47-48
giving directions for, 67, 84-85
Guided Discovery, 63-70, 78, 81-82
Guided Involvement, 71
in Great Britain, 17, 66-67
Inquiry-Discussion, 60-63, 78, 81-82
Lecture, 70-71
Lecture-Discussion, 57-59, 78
logistics for, 83-84
organization for, 51
outline preparation for, 52-55
tour preparation, 81-82, 137
problems, 18, 85-88
random, 71
recommendations for, Table II
school projects for, 46, 66
social awareness during, 35
student problems, 86-87
arranging time in, 81-82
waiting for, 82
warm-ups, 58, 61, 67, 82
workshops, 46

UNESCO, 15

Verbal communication
enunciation, 125
posture and the voice, 124
posture, 126
sentence structure, 123
Victoria and Albert Museum, 11, 13
Visitors
argumentative, 127
illness, 88
interference from, 87
fringe, 86
talking by, 87
uninvited, 86
uninterested, 87
see also Audiences; Groups
Volunteer
art museum, 19
guides, 3
motives, 4, 8
see also Guides
Vukelich, R., 72

Wertz, L. E., 15
Whitman, N. A., 63
Williamsburg, Virginia, 20, 44
Winner, T., 117
Winstanley, B. R., 11
Wittrock, M. C., 65
Woodbury Museum, Margaret, 44
WPA, 13

Young adults, 104-105
Young children, 94-95